Living
in the YES!

Experiencing True Intimacy With God

Laura Jenkins Boal

What People Are Saying

Living in the YES! is much more than a well-written Christian book. It is an invitation into an encounter with the goodness of God, one that calls you by name into a family and empowers you to live in the full measure of life that He has for you.

–Jeremy Springer, Pastor, Arise Birmingham

Laura Boal shares her story and those of others overcoming their physical and emotional Goliaths. Then she hands you the stones you'll need to overcome your own. This book empowers, edifies and encourages, calling each of us closer to Jesus.

–Rev. Kevin Lyons, M.Div., New York

Living in the YES! has one goal: helping you to feel breathtakingly close to the Father—as though you're sitting in the very lap of God.

–CB, Student

It feels like I'm having coffee with a friend. You're sharing my issues and then walking together with me, out of the problem and into the answer. *–CD, Homemaker*

God feels closer and accessible in a way I've never felt before. *–AZ, Schoolteacher*

The Person she's really introducing is Jesus. *–SB, IT Professional*

For the last six years I have suffered from anxiety and massive panic attacks. Then I was introduced to *Living in the YES!* Things are different because of how I'm connecting to God, and my sickness is gone! *–KF, Shipping Manager*

Living in the YES!

Read this book if you dare, but be warned: after you read it, you won't be the same. Thank you for making Jesus tangible in a way that is easily digestible, tasty to the tongue, and overwhelmingly powerful. – *KT, Entrepreneur*

I have known the author for over twenty years. She really is that excited about knowing God and being known by Him. Anyone who reads her book or hears her speak will be drawn into a better, deeper, more real connection with the Lord.
–*JO, Massage Therapist*

I feel such overwhelming kindness and generosity coming through every page. Now I can see what it looks like when someone IS living in the YES, and I'm asking God for more. –*MM, Attorney*

Who Should Read This Book?

This book is all about possibilities.

It's definitely NOT a self-help book. I won't tell you how to work harder, act smarter, and forge your own path to a great life. On the other hand, though... If you're just about tired of your big, bad "self" and you're ready to break through to a bigger, wider kind of life, then you might just stick around, because things are about to get pretty exciting.

You see, life may seem pretty good on its own.
But real life starts with knowing God, deeply and intimately.
That's where the juice comes from, and there's nothing else like it.

God is bigger, better, wiser, kinder, and *gooder* than any of us can ever truly, fully know. He's amazing! And he loves you so much. **Real life**, and I mean a kind of life most of us have never even dreamed of, starts happening when we learn how to live in response to that amazing fact.

It's like God is constantly calling your name
with love, affection and joy.
And your whole being becomes your answer... "YES."

That's what this book is about: knowing God better and drawing closer to him. Letting him write on the pages of your story. It's quite an adventure!

Living in the YES!

Now, this book is written **about** Christians, but it's **for** everybody. In the Bible, God makes amazing promises to those who are "in Christ." And this book is about those people, and how we can live into those promises. But I'm not going to bore you by saying over and over, "*if you are in Christ.*" Just know that it's in there. That's the prequalification. It's how you get in on the ground floor.

What if you're not a Christian? (I know some wonderful people who aren't Christians.) If you want to know more about what God is like, how you can connect with him and live in response to him, this book is still for you. Check it out. See what you think. You can activate these promises for yourself at any time... we'll talk about it afterwards.

Are you human and breathing? Then I know these things are true:
God created you, and he loves you.

He has such good plans for you! Read on to find out more.

Dedication

This book is dedicated to all my brothers and sisters who are standing on the banks of the River, looking out at the flow and thinking, "I don't know. Should I try putting a toe in?"

And it's especially for the prodigals. Father says that he loves you. It's time to come home.

Thank you!

Thank you to Greg and Michelle Haswell, and to the leaders and members of Northlands Church. This isn't just my story, it's your story too. I hope I've told it well.

Christie Corrigan, Jewell McMorris, Joy Oliver. You were so there for me, and this book wouldn't have happened without you. Wow, just wow. Joe Schlosser of Excellent Adventures!, Inc., thanks for so generously sharing your considerable expertise in publishing and media. Also, thanks to ALL the people who gave me interviews, both in and out of print; to my magnificent Focus Group; and to all the other test readers and proofreaders who took part in this project. Each of you sacrificed your time and opened your heart to help make this truth available to others. Many hands have touched this work besides mine, and I am profoundly grateful. Everybody needs to know that.

And a huge, heartfelt thank you to all of the friends and family members who helped, supported, and encouraged me during the long years when I was living with a brain injury, especially my husband Bob and my sister Sally Hoover. I appreciate you more than words can say! At first, it looked like I had wrecked my life on the day when I climbed into that car. I was just so glad that I still had all of you. Then God got all up in the middle of things. Who could have imagined what he had in store?

Living in the YES!

ISBN: 978-0-9915389-0-4

LauraBoal.com

LivingInTheYES.com

Front Cover Design: JoeSchlosser.net

Cover Photo by: Rio Hodges on Unsplash

Contents

List of Connections

Foreword

By Leif Hetland

Founder and President, Global Mission Awareness
Author of *Called to Reign* and *Giant Slayers*

There is room for you at the Father's table, and there's room for you in his great heart. That is the central message of this powerful new book by Laura Boal. In it, she shares her own story, and many other stories as well. She and her contributors talk very honestly about the real problems they faced, and the reasons why they once kept God at a distance. Then they tell us how truly knowing him has transformed their lives. They show us what real intimacy with God looks like, and how it changes us.

The truth she shares is simple, yet profound. It goes beyond mere intellectual curiosity and draws us in at a deeper level. Scriptures leap off the page and come to life, touching us with the living Presence of God. We see prayer as something that happens when our hearts connect with our good Father, so that we can receive his bountiful love. These are not "disciplines." They are delights. They are the product of intimacy, and the birthright of every believer.

Because of what Jesus did, we get to be so much more than God's faithful servants. Instead, we can know what it's like to be his very own, much-loved children; and he wants no child to be left behind. As his children, we get to experience his faithfulness, goodness, kindness, and love, even in the most difficult of circumstances. That is what Laura calls "Living in the YES."

Living in the YES!

Laura learned these truths over many years, while she was dealing with great difficulties. Her pastor is my good friend, and as it happens, I was there in her church on the day when she shared the amazing story of how God had just healed her completely. I saw everyone come to their feet with a roar because they were so overwhelmed with what God had done. It was such a beautiful display of his nature.

Join me now in listening to her story of intimacy and love, poured out all over her again and again, straight from the heart of God. As you read this book I think you will find, as I did, the Father's heart made plain. I think you will feel his transforming love. As she says, these gifts aren't just for her. They are for all of us.

There's just one thing left to say: Welcome to the YES!

Introduction

By Greg Haswell

Senior Pastor, Northlands Church

When Laura and Bob first came to our church several years ago, they were hard-pressed and emotionally bruised from full-on contact with life. They sought God and embraced the beautiful depths and fullness of the Gospel. As they did, we watched them grow into people of great faith, whose lives and stories spread love and grace everywhere they go.

We know Laura's story is true because we witnessed her testimonies firsthand. Although her sufferings were considerable, she never lost hope that God would restore her. While she was waiting, she found out that she could still live connected to Him, and she says that one simple fact changed everything. She's a living, breathing example that it should be the most natural thing in the world for every believer to hear from God, and to truly know Him.

It is my honor to introduce you to a sincere lady whose life demonstrates the fact that NOTHING is impossible with God. As you listen to her story, remember that God has plans for you, too, and they truly are far beyond anything you could ask or imagine. As we often say around here, "There is a giant of a God in you, and He dreams great dreams for you."

Let her words minister to you as you take them to heart. Grace and peace to you in abundance.

Living in the YES!

Chapter 1:

Searching

For The

YES!

Discover the truth that will change your life!

I can't wait to tell you what I've learned about living in the YES!

Living in the YES. It's an amazing place to be... and a different way to live. Here in the YES, we find that our lives have meaning and purpose, and we discover what it feels like to be fully alive. We're surrounded by possibilities and filled with hope. We find real joy that washes away our sadness, and life-giving love that conquers our fears.

Sometimes life can be messy, and whole storms of difficulty may rage outside of us. But when we're living in the YES, those difficulties don't get to come inside our hearts or minds anymore, because the powerful peace within us stills every storm. Even the tough times are better here, as we suddenly realize that our greatest challenges have now become our grandest adventures. When we're living in the YES, no situation seems truly hopeless...and even miracles are possible.

All of that happens when we're connected to the presence of God.

Connecting to God's presence is like getting plugged into the ultimate power source in the universe. You're getting direct downloads of real *life*. It's what we were made for!

Living in the YES!

Once you experience living in the YES—living in God's presence—you can't imagine living any other way.

That's not a "blue sky" promise. It's for real, and it's God's gift to you, purchased at great cost because of the way that he loves you.

God's YES: Why do we need it?

Sometimes in life, it seems like we're surrounded by NO's. They're the really hard problems, the difficult circumstances and disappointments that come our way. The NO's can be hard to deal with, and over time, they can wear us down. Even the strongest, most diligent, most resourceful among us eventually run into problems we can't fix, feelings we don't want to face, or losses we don't know how to handle. That's when we realize how desperately we need God's YES.

Is there a NO in your life right now? Maybe it's a scary medical diagnosis, or a difficult job, or a relationship that's not going so well. Or maybe things are going great for you, and you simply want to experience the most, best life that you can. In either case, take heart! God is speaking his YES over you right now. It's thundering through the heavens. Can you hear it? I can't promise you exactly how things will turn out, but I can assure you that God loves you, he's right there with you, and he is faithful. He's actively working to bring his amazing goodness into your life. The Bible assures us:

"No matter how many promises God has made, they are 'Yes' in Christ." (2 Corinthians 1:20, NIV)

It's time for each of us to add our "Amen."
Yes, Lord! So be it!

How do we find it?

People take so many different paths in their search for a good life. Should you work harder? Think smarter? Go all in for a makeover, or go all out to make better connections? Maybe money or talent will do it, or maybe it's going to be all about power. Maybe you'll go after that big promotion... or maybe you'll give it all up, and go after serenity.

But you can't find the best kind of life in any of those ways.

You can't find it by learning "more rules" or "better guidelines." It isn't about trying harder. It isn't about achieving enlightenment, either. You can't scrabble and claw your way up to this kind of life. You can't work hard enough to do it, can't think your way through it, can't meditate your way into it. Instead, it's a pure gift! And it's already right there, waiting for you, hidden away in God's presence. The only thing you can do is turn to him, receive it, and start living in response to it. [1]

Now, that truly is the adventure of a lifetime.

Going up the mountain

Imagine we're all starting out on a journey together. We're at the foot of a mountain trail—a whole big group of us. Most of us plan on going up the mountain, though some folks expect to stay right here, down in the park. They're bringing out picnic baskets and pushing a friend in an all-terrain wheelchair. As for the rest of us, the biggest group is taking the easy path. Just a few people are taking the trail for hard-core hikers. A couple of folks even brought ropes, spikes, and other climbing gear. They'll attempt to scale the summit.

But you never know what's going to happen when you're on a mountain.

Some of us, climbing the easy trail, get pinned down by a thunderstorm. There we are, wedged into a cleft in the rock, desperately clinging to each other as thunder booms overhead.

Others get stopped by a huge boulder that's blocking the path. One fearless sort scrambles over it, only to be stymied by a rockfall. "We can go forward," he calls back. "But we'll really have to take it slow. The footing over here isn't very sure."

Another group gets sidetracked, and they lose the path entirely. They're slowly picking their way through the wilderness... until, suddenly, they can't go any further. What on earth happened? There must have been a terrible mudslide years ago. Now, this whole part of the mountain is just gone. There is no way forward.

Life can be like that for all of us, can't it? We find ourselves facing obstacles, challenges, even impossibilities. Some of them you can overcome. Others, you can't. Some will just plain wear you down. That's when you realize that life isn't fun anymore. You've lost the sun, lost your way, and maybe even lost all hope of ever finding home again.

God is coming down!

Which part of that mountain are you on right now? Does your life feel like a picnic, or does it feel more like you've gotten caught in a thunderstorm? Is something blocking your path, or is the path gone entirely? Maybe it seems like you're inching along a narrow ledge and your footing is treacherous. Or maybe you're standing on the summit, gazing in wonder over endless miles of valley below.

Wherever you are, it's time look up; because God is coming down.

"Make the crooked road wide and straight for our God. Where there are steep valleys, treacherous descents, raise the highway; lift it up; bring down the dizzying heights. Fill in the potholes and gullies, the rough places. Iron out the shoulders flat and wide.

The Lord will be, really be, among us. The radiant glory of the Lord will be revealed. All flesh together will take it in. Believe it. None other than God, the Eternal, has spoken." (Isaiah 40:3-5, VOICE)

Just stop for a minute and let that soak in. How does it move your heart? *God, the Eternal One, has spoken.* And check it out! He's revealing his intentions toward his people. He doesn't merely want to "meet" with you every once in a while. Instead, he wants to BE with you from now on.

No matter where you are on that mountain, God will find you, and he will help you. He will BE the impossible; he will DO the impossible. He'll do whatever it takes to come for you. NOTHING can keep him apart from his children. So consider this his personal invitation. You can experience his presence and live in his YES. *Right here. Right now!*

My story

I learned about living in the YES when I was in the middle of the worst NO of my life. In 2013 a car wreck left me with a traumatic brain injury that rocked my world. Suddenly everyday life was so hard! I couldn't do the most ordinary things anymore, and I felt confused and overwhelmed most of the time. Before the accident, I'd thought I was valuable because of all the things I could do. Afterwards, almost all of that was gone. A lot of the things that had made me, "me," had simply vanished. It looked like life, as I had known it, was basically over.

That's when God taught me how to live in his YES.

That was amazing! It was like he unlocked the door to a whole new kind of life—one that didn't depend on my connections, abilities, efforts, or achievements. No limitation could stop it. No crisis could block it. No matter what challenges I was facing, I found out that I could still have a good life *right then*, because God was still *right there*. Once I realized that was true, I started worrying less about what I could do and what I couldn't do. I was too busy being loved by God, and finding out what he and I could do together.

As it turns out, you see, I wasn't just a limited person.
I was a limited person connected to an unlimited God.
That's when things started to get exciting.

In the middle of my crisis, God lifted his grace and kindness off the pages of a book and knitted them into my flesh, blood, and bone. Sure, life with a brain injury was still hard. In a lot of ways, though, I actually started living a much better kind of life, because I'd become truly, deeply connected to him. It was such a massive gift that, if he hadn't ever done anything else for me, I could have spent the rest of my life celebrating.

But then God did so much more. Three and a half years after the accident, he healed me completely! That afternoon, I still had all the symptoms of a brain injury. That evening, while I was busy talking to someone else, focusing on them and praying for them … suddenly it felt like God himself had stepped into the room with us, and that's when everything changed.

Other people who were there said it was like watching a massive wave of power pass through my body, and into the person I was praying for. Then, all at once, I didn't have a brain injury anymore! *Every sheared neural connection. Every delayed reaction. All of it was healed in an instant.* The pure wonder of that still overwhelms me. The only thing I'm left with, from that long, dark time, is the extreme joy of knowing how to live in God's YES. And that, of course, is what I want to share with you.

Looking back, I have to laugh out loud. Do you want to know what was the worst limitation I ever faced? It actually wasn't the brain injury. It was the way I'd been trying, for all the years before the wreck, to do life on my own. Living connected to God just really is that much better!*

This is for everyone

What about you? I'm sure you're busy with your own life, and you have your own ups and downs and challenges to deal with. In the middle of all that stuff, can you find your way to God's YES, as well?

I absolutely believe that you can.

You're going to hear that message again and again, and not just from me. You're also about to meet Jo, Selim, Ian and Stefanie; Ellen, Rachel, Vijay; and a whole host of others. They're all real people I

---

* You can read more about my story on page 225.

know, who were facing very real problems. And you're getting a front-row seat, because they're all going to open up and tell you what *actually happened* in their lives... when God showed up.

My friends and I have all been changed—and we're still being changed—because we've been touched by God's presence. We've discovered that the most ordinary lives become extraordinary when we're connected to him. He has done so much for each of us, and we believe he wants to do the same sorts of things for you.

What about you? Maybe you know God well, or maybe you hardly know him. Either way, as we open our hearts and share our stories, we hope you'll be encouraged to know him better. -

Get ready to be blown away! No matter how big you already think God is, or how much you already believe that he loves you... he is MUCH bigger and better than that, and he loves you WAY more.

What can you expect?

In this book, you're going to hear real-life stories from real people. Then we'll use their stories as a springboard, launching us forward as we look for answers to several very important questions.

The adventure begins with our first question: *What is God really like?* The Bible says that he's good. But can we count on that? Is his nature truly an anchor for us, even when everything else in life is likely to change? That's such a big deal! I think it's actually the single most important thing you're ever going to know.

That first answer propels us forward into the next section, as we explore how God relates to us. *Is he still good, even when life feels bad? And what does he really want from us, anyway?* This section caps off with a spectacular truth, as we consider: *Is God calling us to be family servants, or inviting us to be family members?*

Then we'll look at some of the really big things God has done for us. Have you ever done things that you're sorry for but can't undo? Have you ever wondered, as I did, if there was a cure for your own broken-ness? Have you wished you knew how to plug into the real power source, so you can actually experience the richer, better, more abundant life that Jesus promised? These answers continue to amaze me. The Lord doesn't just leave us to struggle through life on our own, and his powerful provisions for us truly are astounding.

Finally, after all of that, we'll be ready to dig deep into the last question. *What in the world is going to happen when all this truth starts coming to life...in us?* The Lord assures each of us that we are significant. Whether we're rich and famous—or not—our lives really do matter. When we're truly, deeply connected to his presence, we find that it's so. Good things start happening around us, things that we couldn't have even imagined before. That's just what it's like when we live in his YES.

These are the truths that changed my life. That was the miracle for me, long before God brought about the other miracle of healing my brain. It was like getting an all-access pass to a life of wonder. And it even worked on the worst days, when it felt like my brain was all but offline. It's important for you to know that. No matter what challenges you're facing, all of this is completely available to you, as well.

As you read this book, I hope you find that the words leap off the page as if they're written, not merely with ink, but also with fire. May

15

they cause your own heart to burn within you, as you have a personal encounter with God and his amazing, transforming love. May you get a fresh connection with his presence as he breaks down barriers and removes roadblocks, bringing you real joy and hope and life.

Impossible becomes possible

As these powerful truths take root in our hearts, we find that we're turning to God from a place of safety and security. We may still face many NO's in life, but we suddenly realize that we're not dealing with them alone anymore. And we find that God's YES is more real, more true, and more powerful than any NO we'll ever face.

How does that work? Sometimes God intervenes and changes our circumstances. Sometimes, instead, he changes us. But either way, more and more, we discover that our lives are being defined by his YES, his love and affirmation and approval that's roaring over us in the face of any other adversity. We learn, more and more, how to partner with the Lord as we "do life" together. We begin to understand what the Bible actually means when it says that God is "for" us... and *nothing* is impossible for him.

The Lord wants to explode every single barrier that's been preventing us from truly, deeply knowing him. As he does, we start bringing down our own walls and really letting him in. That's when we look up in wonder and realize: *HE is here. Right here. Right now!* And in his presence, we become changed from the inside out.

It's as if we start breathing in the very air of heaven. Then, as we breathe out—as we start living differently, living in response to his amazing truth—the world around us starts changing, too. [2]

Finding more and better life

In John 10:10 (MSG), Jesus says, "I came that they can have real and eternal life, more and better life than they ever dreamed of."

Real and eternal life?
More and better life than we ever dreamed of?

That's not just the promise of Heaven. It's the kind of life God offers us *right now*. He purchased it, at great cost, because of his overwhelming love for us. I believe he wants every one of us to enjoy this priceless gift.

Will you come along on the journey? We're going to explore some amazing territory as we talk about living in God's YES. Here's the bottom line: We get to know God. We can actually be connected to him! If you truly want to experience the most, best life that you can, it really is that simple.

All the life is in him.
Want more life?
Get more connected.

These truths are so big, so wonderful, and so powerful that only God could have dreamed this up! I suppose we could call them "mysteries," because they blow our minds and transform our thinking. But they're certainly not secrets! They're for all of us.

Are you ready?
What adventure does God have in store for you?

Recap: Living in the YES

God wants so much more for us than we want for ourselves. And he's gone to great lengths to make sure we can *actually experience* all that he's bought for us. Life can be messy, and sometimes it feels like we're surrounded by NO's. Yet God's presence with us is the ultimate YES. That fact is more real than any NO we'll ever face. It truly has the power to change our lives.

These are the wonderful realities we're going to explore:

- God is truly good.
- He isn't mad at me.
- I don't have to earn his love.
- He welcomes me into his family.
- I am really forgiven.
- He has given me his righteousness.
- I can live connected to him.
- My life matters!

What are "Connections?"

What would it be like if you and I could *actually see* spiritual realities with our own eyes? What if we could touch them with our hands? If we could see the glory of God; if we could visibly approach the Gates of Heaven in prayer; what would that be like?

"Connections" are little stories you'll find scattered throughout the book. They're meant to help you envision such spiritual realities as if they're concrete and real (because they are.) They're based on Bible verses. Some involve speculation. You'll need to engage your imagination—or, possibly, to see with the eyes of your spirit.

Consider them a personal invitation for you to connect with the Lord.

Here's what I'm praying over you…

"That the light of God will illuminate the eyes of your imagination [or, the eyes of your heart], flooding you with light, until you experience the full revelation of the hope of his calling."
(Ephesians 1:18, TPT)

Connection: Want To Come Along?

Have you ever read a Bible story and imagined what it would be like if you were actually there?

Imagine you're living in Bible times. You've been walking towards a friend's place and you pause to rest for a bit, enjoying the sunny spring day, looking at the new growth and feeling the warm breeze. You're watching a group of people as they come towards you, laughing easily and talking energetically with each other. They look really happy. As they draw near to you, suddenly the leader stops them all.

That has to be HIM!

You've heard about this Jesus. They say he isn't like the other teachers. He's real, and kind, and he helps people. So many stories. There was the Samaritan woman at the well; even her own people wouldn't have anything to do with her. Zacchaeus, the despicable tax collector who collaborated with the Romans. The woman Amara[3], brought before the rulers to be stoned to death because she was caught in adultery. And more!

They say Jesus talked to every one of them as if they mattered. They say he knows things about you that you've never told anybody. He looks at you as if he really sees you, and once he does, you're never the same.

And now he's here. He's turning towards you!

Nobody has ever looked at you like that. It's as if he sees the real you, and you see acceptance and warmth in his eyes. He gestures at the road ahead. "We were just on our way into town," he says with a grin. "Want to come along?"

"Weren't we excited when he talked with us on the road and opened up the meaning of the Scriptures for us?"   Luke 24:32 (GW)

Chapter 2:

God

Is Truly

Good

Laura

What is God really like?

That's the most important thing you're ever going to know. People can say crazy things about God. They'll say he "allowed" sickness to teach them a lesson - yet his name means: "I AM HEALER." They'll say he sends hurricanes to punish cities - yet Jesus stilled every storm he was in. It's like the party game, "Gossip." We invent explanations for things we don't understand. Our ideas get further and further from the truth, and we don't realize it. That kind of misinformation spreads like wildfire, destroying everything in its path.

But God isn't like that. It's time to set aside our preconceptions and misperceptions. Come discover the real truth about the One who made you, the One who will help, heal, and sustain you. The Bible is remarkably consistent at declaring who God is. Its eyewitness accounts keep telling us the same things, over and over. Modern day eyewitnesses? They say that words alone can't tell half the story.

God says that we can know him.
And knowing him? That changes everything.

What is God really like?

Have you ever been awed by majesty? I have.

A few years back, my husband Bob and I were traveling through Colorado with friends when we decided to take a quick shortcut. It was just a little dotted line on the map. I don't know why we thought that sounded like a good idea, deep in the mountains in the middle of winter; but at any rate, it's what we did. And suddenly, we found ourselves crawling like tiny ants across the massive surface of a giant mountain.

It was unbelievable! We quickly began to wonder if our "little dotted line" had been one of the *actual cart tracks* used by gold miners in the 1800s, because it must have been cut for a mule rather than a car. For twenty-five miles we inched along a deeply rutted one-lane dirt road, plowing through frequent snow drifts and going extra slow on the icy parts. Immediately on our left rose a forbidding cliff of sheer granite. I peered up out of the window and could barely see the sky, far above. Immediately on our right, the cliff fell straight down, just as steeply and just as far. *No shoulder. No guard rails!*

On we went, sharply twisting left and right as this tiny cart track clung to the side of that imposing mountain. Then we inched through a long, narrow tunnel, burrowing straight through the living rock, and over a rickety wooden bridge that rattled as if it couldn't possibly carry the weight of our old, heavy car.

I'd heard that the Rockies were big. But believing in them was nothing like getting up close and personal with their spectacular, jaw-dropping, eye-popping reality. I suppose you could say that I *encountered* the mountain on the road that day, and it pretty much changed everything I thought I knew about mountains.

It's like that with God. Whatever we think we know about him, he's so much more! He's utterly magnificent and glorious. He's both heart-stoppingly wonderful and absolutely terrifying. Don't you dare just sit back and let someone else tell you what he's like. You really need to know him—and relate to him— for yourself.

> *It's time to come closer.*
> *Closer.*
> *Closer still!*
> *When you do…*
> *What will you find is true?*

God doesn't change

That's the first and best thing we need to know about God: *He doesn't change.* It's really hard for us to take that in, because we're changing all the time. You can change your clothes or change your mind. You can even have a change of heart! Circumstances change, lifestyles change, people change. In this world, things are always changing.

But not God.

Nothing about God ever fails, shifts or changes. Nothing ever could! He never needs an upgrade. He's entirely whole, perfect, and complete. His wonderful creativity produces endless variations. But they're only going to display, never contradict, the glorious riches of his boundless nature.

All that God is, he is absolutely; and all that he does is going to proceed from all that he is. *He is altogether powerful. He's absolutely holy. He's entirely faithful, loving, and good.* He is all those things, all the time, unfailingly. Our own lives are variable and impermanent. We can't always count on other people. We can't even always count on ourselves! We can make quite a mess of our own lives, or we can get stuck in a mess that somebody else made. But even then—no matter what happens—God's vast, eternal nature remains unchanged and undiminished; and he says that his heart is always turned towards us.

Do you need to know that? Then let these powerful, living words wash over you. Drink in their strength:

"God is not a man—He doesn't lie. God isn't the son of a man to want to take back what He's said, or say something and not follow through, or speak and not act on it...Every good gift bestowed, every perfect gift received comes to us from above, courtesy of the Father of lights. He is consistent. He won't change His mind or play tricks in the shadows." (Numbers 23:19, James 1:17, VOICE)

That's such good news! No matter what happens, God is still perfect, whole, and unchanging. We can count on that. We may not be entirely sure what he's going to do, or how, or when. But that kind of "not knowing" doesn't matter so much, once we understand that we truly can trust his heart.

Awed by his majesty

Simply "believing in God" couldn't begin to prepare us for the mind-blowing reality of his presence. The Bible describes him as majestic, wonderful, and powerful beyond anything we can comprehend. He's eternal, immense, and vast, and he's far more substantial and *real* than we are. His words alone carry such force that ages ago, as God said, *"Let there be light..."*, the very Universe itself exploded into existence. *Every atom still vibrates. The Universe keeps expanding. Are they still responding to the sound of his voice?*

Just think about Moses. Sure, he believed in God; but his whole world changed on the day when the two of them actually met. Moses was simply minding his own business, quietly tending sheep, when suddenly God was *right there*. And what about Isaiah? Did he think it was going to be a typical day? *"I saw the Lord,"* he recounts with amazement, *"high and exalted, seated on a throne; and the train of his robe filled the temple... the doorposts and thresholds shook and the temple was filled with smoke."* Both of them were completely overwhelmed.

David, too, was utterly awed by the immensity of God's presence. His joy spills out in Psalms like this one: "Make music for the one who strides the ancient skies. Listen to his thunderous voice of might split open the heavens... he alone has all the strength and power! Proclaim his majesty! For his glory shines down... His mighty strength soars in the clouds of glory. God, we are consumed with awe, trembling before you as your glory streams from your Holy Place." (Psalm 68:33-35, TPT)

The "Awe Effect" even happened to Daniel. As a seasoned prophet, he was used to hearing the voice of God. Yet he felt completely undone when he encountered God's actual presence. "I was terrified," he admits frankly.[4]

What would it be like if YOU encountered God like that?

When that happens, I think each of us will be completely over-whelmed and utterly undone. A moth might as well try to dance with a burning flame! And the Bible says that each of us will, in fact, meet him one day. If it's not here in this life, then we will certainly encounter him after death. Our strength will give way and we'll all fall flat on our faces. We too will be totally awed as we come face to face with God and his immense, burning, fiery glory.

Drawn by his love

While we're shocked and awed by God's overwhelming majesty, we're also irresistibly drawn by his wild, tender love for us. *God is love!*[5] Love is not just what he does; it's who he is. And his love is so much *more* than our own. No words can describe it. It isn't vague or general. It's so much more than, "Aww, I just love everybody." His love is real and true and personal. It's immense, intense, and life-giving.

Have you ever felt lost or anonymous?
Then you need to know the truth.
God sees YOUR face. He hears YOUR voice. He loves YOU!

When you experience that kind of love, it completely redefines you. Just think what it does to Saul of Tarsus. He's one of the rising stars in the religious world of his day, but his heart is so cold. He's going from town to town, killing Christians, determined to stamp out their kind... no matter how much suffering he causes.

Then Saul meets the resurrected Jesus, and he is transformed.

From that point on, his heart is on fire. He says: "All the things I once thought were so important are gone from my life... I've dumped it all in the trash so that I could embrace Christ and be embraced by him... I gave up all that inferior stuff so I could know Christ personally." And listen to what he calls down on us: "...The extravagant dimensions of Christ's love. Reach out and experience the breadth! Test its length! Plumb the depths! Rise to the heights! Live full lives, full in the fullness of God."   (Philippians 3:8-10, Ephesians 3:18-19, MSG)

My friend "Selim" says he knows firsthand what it's like to experience that kind of love. He was pacing the floor, distraught, as his wife "Yasmin" lay dying in the hospital. *That's when Jesus literally walked through the wall and came to Selim.* Jesus told Selim what to do. He promised that Yasmin would live, and she did.

Selim says that he knew he was in the presence of God—because he was in the presence of Love personified. He was changed in an instant, immediately becoming a Christ-follower as that amazing, overwhelming love washed over him.

Amazed by his faithfulness

Does God always keep his promises? Some people wonder about that, especially if they've prayed for a long time without getting an answer. Does God ever put all his calls on hold and just go fishing?

For instance, think about the life of Joseph.[6] God tells Joseph that he's going to become a great man, and Joseph tells everybody. His brothers don't like that. They decide to take Joseph's fate into their own hands. They kidnap him, talk about murdering him, and then sell him to slave traders. He ends up in a strange country, serving a life sentence in prison for a crime he didn't commit. If anybody's ever had a right to think that God let them down, I guess it would be Joseph.

Joseph certainly has plenty of time, sitting in prison, to be mad at God. Maybe he also reflects on his own mistakes. Maybe he thinks about all the people who've let him down. Maybe it feels like he's never gotten a break in life. But even if he starts out by thinking about those things, he clearly doesn't get stuck there. Instead, Joseph chooses to *really live* the life that's in front of him. He keeps turning to God, and he keeps calling on God's faithfulness. That much is obvious from the things he says and does, and from the choices he makes. And he lives like that for years.

The end of Joseph's story, of course, astounds us all. His skills and his character grow. Eventually, he turns into such a gifted administrator that he operates the whole prison, from the inside. He learns how business gets done in Egypt. Then, at a crucial moment in history, Joseph becomes the second most powerful man in the country. He saves large parts of the known world from a global famine. In time, he even saves his brothers. He basically tells them: "Hey, guys, that thing you did? I know that you meant to hurt me, but just look at all the good that God brought out of it!" [7]

At first, it really didn't look like Joseph was going to be the poster boy for God's faithfulness. Yet God was still so faithful! God's heart was just way bigger than anybody could've imagined. He didn't only want to save Joseph. He wanted to save a whole lot of people. So instead of writing his faithfulness into Joseph's circumstances, God wrote his faithfulness into Joseph's heart. *Because of that, Joseph gets to do far more than just experiencing a breakthrough. He gets to become a breakthrough.*

That's something we all need to remember the next time things go sideways. God has the most amazing way of working his powerful goodness and faithfulness into our lives, even in the face of truly dreadful, seemingly "impossible" circumstances. He remembers his promises and keeps them, not only within our lifetimes but across generations. "Even if we are faithless," the Bible promises, "he never wavers in his faithfulness to us!" (2 Timothy 2:13, TPT)

Awash in his goodness

God is entirely good. He's never bitter, short-tempered, or moody. He could never conceive of, or act on, evil intentions. Instead, he's patient and kind, and a massive river of *life* flows constantly from his presence. If you're involved in a heart-to-heart relationship with God, he's always sending that river your way. Even if he rebukes you, it's only ever going to be redeeming. Those are the moments when he's cleaning you up, correcting your course, and putting you back to rights. That's just what God is like. He's good!

God's goodness wasn't only real in Bible times. He still writes his goodness on our hearts and makes it real in our lives *today*. He still helps and heals people. He still gives sight to blind eyes and makes crippled legs whole. He sets people free from depression, anorexia, and addictions. He brings hope, healing, and deep meaning to our lives. I actually know people who know him like that, and you're going to be hearing from some of them.

Remember what Jesus says he wants for each of us: *Real life...more and better life than we ever dreamed of.*[8] He's talking about God's real, true, joy-bringing, life-giving, strength-inducing, full-on-empowering goodness. And he's giving us full access! That's what starts warming our hearts the moment we draw closer to him.

So what if you're in a committed relationship with God, and your life circumstances aren't lining up with his essential nature? *Then you get to ask him to come, and I believe that he will.* He assures us, "I will never leave you alone, never! And I will not loosen my grip on your life!" [9]

Your story doesn't have to be over until God shows up and does something completely amazing, either in you, through you, with you, or for you. If that hasn't happened yet, then your story just isn't over. Look up! *God loves you and his heart is "for" you.* Call on his goodness.

Kicking back with God

Picture this: God and Moses have been through quite a lot, leading an unruly bunch of people out of slavery and into a miracle. At last, they finally get a quiet moment to kick back together. The media has gone home. All the cameras are off. It's just the two of them. That's when

Living in the YES!

Moses basically says, "Come on, now, God. I've earned some points here. I want to know the real YOU."

What is God going to say?

"I am the Lord," he answers. "I am the God who is tender and kind. I am gracious. I am slow to get angry. I am faithful and full of love." (Exodus 34:6, NIRV)

> *Hey! Hang on, now. Did you really get that?*
> *Tender and kind.*
> *Gracious.*
> *Faithful and full of love.*
> *That's what God is really like!*

Do you want to know God like that? I sure do. Come with me. Let's take another look at who God says he is.

> *Get ready to be blown away.*

God is ...

- **He's faithful and reliable**. We can count on him.
- **He's loving.**
- **He's good.**
- **He's authentic and trustworthy**. He doesn't say one thing and do another.
- **He doesn't change.** He's the same, yesterday, today, forever.
- **He's powerful** beyond anything we can imagine.
- **He's also gentle** with hurting people.
- **He's compassionate**. He understands our suffering and he will carry it for us.
- **He's full of joy.**
- **His presence is so vast** that it fills the universe.
- **He knows us intimately**. He knew all about us before we were born. He keeps track of all the details about us.
- **He's respectful**. He invites us to join him, but he will not violate our boundaries or ignore our choices.
- **He's fair**. The word we translate as "righteousness" also means real justice. God says that he hates injustice, and he promises that he will make things right by the end. Make it so, Lord!
- **He's not afraid of evil** or threatened by it.
- **His plans are amazing and his methods are effective.** What he wants will ultimately be accomplished.
- **He's never lonely, but he invites us** to know him and be with him.[10]

That's just the beginning of knowing what God is like! The reality of his presence reaches far beyond our human comprehension. His nature is like a rich, multi-patterned tapestry: powerful yet gentle, infinite and also imminent, hating sin while loving sinners. He really is the one true Superhero. I suspect we'll spend eternity transfixed in wonder as we come to know him more and more.

Now I think we're ready to hear Jo's story. I hope you're sitting down.

The day I died and met God

Jo Moody lay bleeding to death in a foreign hospital. First, the surgeon had accidentally nicked her femoral artery. Then her sutures ruptured. By the time her sisters got the attention of the medical staff, it was too late to save her. In those final, terrifying moments, as the doctors and nurses worked frantically over her failing body, she felt unimaginable pain, horror, panic, chaos —and then perfect peace. She says:

"The day I died and met God changed everything.

"One second I was there in my body, and then I wasn't. I was all the way up at the top of the surgical suite, looking down at this unbelievable, bloody mess. I was elated. I was in shock, like, 'Look! I'm free!'

"Then God came for me. His glory was so enormous. I was completely overwhelmed by his presence. To experience the majesty of the Father, the feeling is indescribable. It's like nothing else. Maybe there are some words on the planet that would describe it, but I don't know any in English. I wanted to bow, but I didn't have a body, so I couldn't figure out how to do that. I wanted to shrink away. I was so in awe. But there was also this need to open oneself up to the greatest love. God's heart is so magnificent, and it's given out, not just in pieces but the wholeness of it. I was just dumbfounded by the magnitude of his love and the presence of his majesty.

"I knew he was my Father, he was my savior, he was my lover, he was my best friend. I knew all of that, in emotion as well as mind as well as heart. I knew it all the way through me. And then, when you're with the Lord there's this complete absence of any fear or doubt. There's no way to explain what that feels like. It's a knowing that you know that you know, that everything is true. Everything in the Bible is true. Everything you can know about God, and more than you can know, it's manifest and it's right there. I was in shock. I was awestruck, and I was completely overwhelmed.

"Then he spoke, and his voice was so huge. It went into me and all over me and all around me. It simply filled everything. I don't know what substance a spirit is made of, but it felt like his voice penetrated everything about me, all the way down to a molecular level. It was both awe-inspiring and terrifying, yet so loving. I wasn't afraid. My human brain just couldn't comprehend.

"I didn't have any doubt at all that I was created by this amazing God, for this amazing God, and that I would be with this amazing God forever. I had this absolute assurance. It was like a feeling and a knowing that you could never get on the earth. I just loved him, more than I knew it was possible to love. And all I wanted to do was to be with him, and I never wanted to leave him."

Jo came back for the sake of her little boy, and I'm so glad she did! You can read more of her story on page 236.

The one thing

This side of heaven, most of us won't meet God in such a dramatic way.
But he says that every one of us can truly know him.

YOU can know him.
Right here. Right now!

You can learn his nature. You can see his kindness in action. You can experience his peace and joy, his hope and help, in good times and in tough seasons. Sometimes life can feel harsh, and it brings challenges to all of us; the first lesson in the Bible is that we live in a fallen world. That's when it's especially important to remember *who God is*, and *who he is for you*. He promises that he'll be there with you, no matter what happens. And he offers you the chance to really know him.

Think about Moses kicking back with God.
Then imagine yourself.
Imagine you're right there, with them, in that holy place.

"Whenever, though, [we] turn to face God as Moses did, God removes the veil and there [we] are—face-to-face! [We] suddenly recognize that God is a living, personal presence, not a piece of chiseled stone... Nothing between us and God, our faces shining with the brightness of his face. And so we are transfigured much like the Messiah, our lives gradually becoming brighter and more beautiful as God enters our lives and we become like him."
(2 Corinthians 3:16-18, MSG)

Truly knowing God's goodness. Knowing him as he is, in all his splendor, majesty and love. That's the birthright of all believers. Jesus purchased it for us at great cost—not a cold, dead religion, but a warm, living relationship with the One whose face lights up all of heaven. It's the one thing that matters most in life, the one thing we were made for:

We can know him.

The more we see God as he truly is, the more everything else in life comes into its proper perspective. The tender kindness of his wonderful grace. The infinite strength of his awesome power. His resplendent glory and goodness. His amazing, transforming love. And all of him is leaning towards us; he says that he is for us, not against us.

The Bible says that God himself is the desire of nations.[11] I think Selim and Jo would both agree, don't you? His presence really is the thing that we all long for.

Recap: God is truly good

What is God really like?

No matter what point we're starting from, the Lord invites us to come closer and truly know him. To come so close that our hair stands on end as he displays his awesome strength and glorious majesty. To *actually feel* his endless love for us. To be healed and calmed by his gentle kindness. To be challenged, and to grow, as he shows us how he sees things. The Bible says that God is powerful, holy, faithful, loving, and good. He's amazing! When we see him as he is, we're left speechless. And all we can whisper is, *More, Lord!*

> *Come and know him.*
> *Be awed by majesty.*

Connection: Meeting Jesus

Imagine you're having a dream.
At least, you think it's a dream…

It all feels so real, and the colors look so vivid! You're standing in a dimly lit room with opulent surroundings. Could this be Solomon's temple? Your gaze sweeps around as you eagerly drink in the spectacle.

Then you see Jesus, and everything else just fades away.

Before, you've thought of him as the humble man on the Cross, dying for the sins of the world, and rightly so. Now, you also realize: *he is so much more.* This is God Himself, in all his resurrected glory. He's dressed in pure white and wearing a magnificent, jewel-encrusted breastplate. Its gems flash with a fire that's brighter than the purest diamonds on earth. Yet even their beauty pales when you look into his eyes. There you see power and majesty, glory and strength. His compassion reaches out to you—and you sense a depth that goes far beyond any sadness you could ever bear to know. At the same time, he radiates deep, irresistible joy. His love for you is so tangible that you feel transported in his presence. That's when you think:

This is real life! Everything that happened before was the dream.

Jesus' face shines like the sun. Your eyes become dazzled as you look at him, and the light from his presence casts a shimmering glow in every direction. As he takes your hand, you feel strength and purpose and happiness flooding into your being.

"I didn't know it could be like this," you whisper in wonder.

In his presence you lose track of time.
Has it been five minutes or five years? This is pure joy.

Then the glow gently fades, and you see him in his human form: a friendly Jewish carpenter with dark hair, laughing eyes and work-roughened, nail-scarred hands. He gives your hands a reassuring squeeze.

"Don't go," you plead longingly.
Nothing could ever prepare you to be apart from him again.

He smiles gently. "The time will come," he promises, "but it is not yet. For now, we need to leave Heaven and go back to Earth. Don't worry! I'm sending the Holy Spirit to be with you always. He'll help you to know me better there, so that you can also know me better here."

The glow of Jesus' presence still warms your heart as you awaken. You're in your own room, gazing in wonder at the familiar surroundings as if you're seeing them for the first time. Then you slip into a restful sleep, better and sweeter than any you've ever had before.

He's with me! you think.
Whatever happens, he is here. It's going to be okay.

Then Jesus' appearance was dramatically altered. A radiant light as bright as the sun poured from his face. And his clothing became luminescent... He was transfigured before their very eyes.
Matthew 17:2 (TPT)

Chapter 3:

He Isn't

Mad

At Me

 *Laura*

Come on, now. It happens to all of us.

The problem with having mountaintop experiences in life is that they can be followed by valleys. You know what I mean: you found out that you lost the job. You got the diagnosis. The phone rings and you know it's going to be the news that you're dreading. All at once, the warm afterglow of the mountaintop drains away, and you're suddenly left facing a cold, hard reality.

That's when you may wonder:
Is God still good, even when life feels bad?

Is God still good, even when life feels bad?

Ian says: "Four days after our first child was born, my wife Rozanne suddenly developed a blood infection and died. At first, I didn't know what to do. It was so unexpected. I was in shock and I just felt numb. There I was, not only single again, but a single Dad."

What do you do in a moment like that?
How do you keep going when a nightmare just became your reality?

On hearing Ian's story, you may simply say, "Aw, that's too bad." You may find that your heart aches in sympathy for his pain. Or you may actually know from personal experience what it's like to feel that kind of gut-wrenching, heart-stopping agony, the kind that leaves you fighting for your next breath. Ian puts it like this: "At first you don't think about tomorrow. You just have to get through today."

Living through life's challenges can be hard enough—especially if, like Ian, you're facing a crisis that won't be going away in a few short days or weeks. In moments like that, some people ask: *does God still care about me?* They may even wonder if God is the one who actually caused their problems. In a way, it all boils down to this:

Is God still good?
And will he be good to me?

If you've ever wondered about something like that, take heart! Life on this planet is messy, imperfect, and very fragile, and we all face hard times. But hard times can't hinder God's amazing love for us, and they can't prevent his powerful presence from being real and active in our lives. Even in our toughest moments, we can stay connected to him.

Once we learn that, instead of being crushed by the difficulties of life we can thrive, even in the midst of the most awful chaos. We can emerge stronger, more confident, and more peaceful. Under pressure, we can actually become truer, kinder, and more real, as if the fires of adversity have only burned away our imperfections and left behind our best, truest selves. If the time comes when it feels like you're drowning in wave after wave of difficulty, don't be afraid! I know the One who walks on water, and he loves to make his children drownproof.

There are so many different questions we tend to ask in a crisis.
Let's go after a few answers.

Are you mad at me?

Let's start by exploding the myth that can keep you stuck in tragedy:

God didn't send a crisis to punish you because he wanted to
"pay you back" for something that you did.

People have been mistaking God's intentions like that since ancient times. Maybe it's because that's the sort of thing that they, themselves, would have done. Maybe it's because they've misread or misunderstood the Old Testament Law and the Prophets.[12] But Jesus made his intentions—and his Father's intentions—very clear when he said: "God did not send his Son into the world to judge and condemn the world, but to be its Savior and rescue it!" (John 3:17, TPT)

Tula knows about that. She thought God was angry with her because of the things she'd done. *Then she had an encounter with him.* She explains, "Somehow I'd gotten the idea that God the Father was really angry. I'd thought Jesus was like the good older brother, standing between me and the wrath of God. But that isn't true at all! The Bible says that Jesus is the perfect representation of the Father.[13] Jesus is kind, because God the Father is kind. They're alike." (We'll hear more from Tula later.) That amazing discovery changed her life. It can change yours, as well.

Now of course, if you've done something that's really stupid, dangerous or bad, God will certainly tell you to stop it, and he'll want you to make restitution to the degree that you can. He'll want you to take responsibility for what you've done, and you may face earthly consequences for your actions. If so, he will walk with you step by step and help you.

> *When we ask God, "Are you mad at me?" he reassures us:*
> *I have never, ever stopped loving you.*
> *Come to me; let me comfort you and heal you.*
> *Let me put you to rights, and put things around you to rights.[14]*

Is this your will?

Is everything that happens God's will? As we say in the South, *not hardly.* This world seems to be a muddy place, spiritually, where God's will isn't the only influence at work. For example, he has given every one of us a personal will, and he won't violate our boundaries or ignore our choices.

If you want to know what God's will looks like, though, that's easy. Just look at Jesus. He was the living embodiment of God's will.[15] Here's what he did: he healed everyone who asked. He forgave them. He set them free from every kind of torment and shame, and he gave them dignity, wholeness and joy instead. He invested in people, and if it took time for them to grow, he understood. When it looked like somebody had died too young, he had an astonishing habit of going to funerals and actually raising them from the dead! Even his corrections and rebukes were redeeming, intended to protect the weak and bring life to someone who was headed in the wrong direction.

Think about the sorts of things that Jesus did. Then ask yourself: what would he do if he walked into this room, right now? That's probably a good start on understanding what God really wants for you. My advice is to come to him, ask him for it, and keep asking.[16] Keep looking for his answer. Do what you have the power to do, and then keep praying for a miracle. When we pray and keep praying, the most amazing things seem to happen. God tends to show up, and when he does, he blows our minds.

Did you know that the language of the Lord's Prayer is very forceful? *"Kingdom, come! Will of God, be done! Cause it to be on earth as it is in heaven!"* [17] We're God's children, and he invites us to partner with him. We may or may not have been experiencing God's will at the start of our situation; but we can all come together to call down his will while we're working our way through it.

When we ask God what he really wants for us, he says:
Hold up! Let me strengthen you so you can understand the answer.
My dreams are a whole lot bigger than yours are. [18]

Why is this happening?

All of us have probably asked that particular question, and it's the one that God almost never seems to answer.

I expect we could all give the theoretical explanations about why bad things happen. We can make truly horrible choices without thinking through the consequences. Other people's choices can affect us as well. Mistakes and accidents can happen, and we live in an imperfect, fallen world. Sometimes we suspect the devil is at it again, trying to steal, kill, and destroy. But we may never fully understand all of the reasons why a particular crisis happened. Even if we do, that won't turn back time or reverse a tragedy, nor is it likely to soothe our broken hearts.

If we get stuck in that particular place, where we keep asking "why?" again and again, we need help. (I've needed that kind of help.) Living that way for any length of time works about as well as trying to drive a car while you're only looking at the rearview mirror. Ian says:

"In the beginning there's a tendency to ask, 'Why did this happen to me? Why didn't the Lord prevent it?' I still don't have a great answer to that. But I quickly realized that knowing it wouldn't get me anywhere.

"I had a relationship with the Lord. I knew what it was like to feel his presence and to hear from him. That made it so much easier to deal with the times when my emotions tried to take charge. His promises, even the ones that seemed like they would never be fulfilled, were just as true as they ever were. The Lord is good and he is for my good.

"I came to the point of asking a different kind of question. I'd tell the Lord, 'Okay, I don't know why this happened and I don't need to know. But I do need you to tell me: What comes next? How do I go forward from here? The dreams I've had, your promises over my life, how does all of that work now?'"

God, do you care?

In the last chapter, we talked about God's overwhelming faithfulness, goodness and love. Those are the truest realities in the universe, and they are still true, even in our darkest times. When things in our lives go wrong, is it because God stopped caring about us? Never! "SOMETHING may be going on," we can say with confidence, "but it isn't THAT something." Remember this great promise: "The eyes of the Lord are on the righteous, and his ears are attentive to their cry." (Psalm 34:15, NIV) God's heart is for you. He's always paying attention to what's going on with you, and he always cares.[19]

The Bible says that when we suffer, God's heart is moved with compassion for us.[20] That's a shocking statement, because "compassion" can only be described as *gut-wrenching pain*. It means actually feeling someone's pain, exactly as they experience it. Listen to Alex's story. (You need to know, now, that Alex is not a weepy sort of person.)

"After church one Sunday," he says, "I saw a group of people praying for Miss Julia in her wheelchair, and I thought I'd join them. As I got closer to them, suddenly, out of the blue I got hit by this really heavy sense of hopelessness and abandonment and frustration. I started sobbing uncontrollably and I couldn't stop. Later, I asked the Lord what that was about. He told me Miss Julia had felt pain like that for years, and that he felt all of it. He said nothing can happen to any of us, without his feeling exactly what we're feeling. And there was more! I didn't only feel God's pain. I felt his heart for her. I knew that he wanted Miss Julia to do more than walk. He wanted her to run.

"It's definitely changed my outlook. There have been plenty of times in my own life when I started to think, 'Where is God, and why is he letting this happen to me?' But then I realize he's right there with me, and he feels it, too. He may not have wished for something to happen, but he's going to be with me to see it through."

That's what God's compassion is like.
He literally knows what it's like to feel our pain.
Keep that in mind as you read this montage of clips from the Bible:

"When he saw the vast crowds of people, Jesus' heart was deeply moved with compassion, because they seemed weary and helpless, like wandering sheep without a shepherd... his heart was deeply moved with compassion toward them, so he healed all the sick who were in the crowd...[He said,] 'I promise that I will never leave you helpless or abandon you as orphans...I am with you every day... I will never leave you alone, never! And I will not loosen my grip on your life!'" (Matthew 9:36, 14:14, John 14:18, Matthew 28:20, Hebrews 13:5, TPT)

Isn't that comforting? God's heart is moved with compassion for YOU. You may face tough times in life, but you're never going to go through them alone. God promises that he will never leave or abandon you; he loves you way too much for that.

> *If we ask, "Where are you? Do you care what's happening?"*
> *God says:I love you, child.*
> *I'm right here with you, and I'm not going anywhere.*[21]

What are you doing?

Whatever is going on in our lives, for whatever reason, God always has plans to bring us good.[22]

Now, in a healthy family, we protect our children tenderly, but we don't want them to act like babies forever. So we teach them. We gradually give them room to explore the world and deal with its challenges. They reach for goals, make mistakes and learn. We watch over them, enjoying their growth, whispering suggestions when necessary. If it looks like they're getting into danger, we'll warn them about it and urge them to stop, and hopefully they'll listen. We'll stand shoulder to shoulder with them if a crisis should happen. God's family works a lot like that, too.[23] The New Testament is clear about it: God doesn't beat us up, but he does grow us up. Just listen to this:

"My fellow believers, when it seems as though you are facing nothing but difficulties see it as an invaluable opportunity to experience the greatest joy that you can! For you know that when your faith is tested it stirs up power within you to endure all things. And then as your endurance grows even stronger it will release perfection into every part of your being until there is nothing missing and nothing lacking." (James 1:2-4, TPT)

I love hearing about the times when God shows up in people's lives, bringing miraculous healing and provision. But those aren't the only miraculous things he does when we're in a crisis. Think about the internal resources someone needs in order to become truly great: things like strength, courage, honesty, kindness, persistence, and faith. Those traits are most often developed and strengthened when we're under pressure. Sometimes, you see, God rescues us out of a situation, and other times he grows and changes us while we're in a situation.

Take heart! I'm certainly not saying that the Lord caused your crisis, but he promises that he will be with you in it. If you turn to him, he'll help you, so that you can come out of it with something very precious that you didn't have before. When it comes to God's children, whatever situation we're facing, he always has an end in mind.[24]

> When we ask the Lord, "What are you doing?" he reassures us:
> I'm right here, helping you.
> I'm making you more whole than ever before.
> One day, you're going to stand with me in glory, and nothing will be
> missing within you, and nothing will be lacking.[25]

Jo Moody: Will you walk with me, Lord?

The hardest part of dealing with difficulty is when it keeps on going. Even the strongest believers can become battle-weary, and we can wonder why God hasn't shown up yet. But that's not the time to give up or give in! That's when we lean on the Lord, every single day.

How do we do it? Jo, from the last chapter, contended for fifteen years before her healing came. Here's what she says:

"When you're in a situation like that, you have to draw closer to God. It's an attitude of turning towards him and leaning on him. You have to know who Christ is. He is our healing, our freedom. He's the true source for our identity, our authority, our power. In all things he is perfect love. He is the Person of Truth, the Prince of Peace. When things happen in my life, or when thoughts come to my mind, that come against that understanding of who Christ is, I don't permit myself to spend a lot of time thinking about them. I actively turn away from them. You can only understand what is true in relation to perfect Truth. You keep turning towards God, minute by minute. You choose to rely on the fact that he's going to be all those things for you. You ask him for help.

"Who is Jesus? Who does he say that I am? Don't deny your pain, but discipline your thought life and choose to focus on that higher truth.

"Most importantly, remember how much you're accepted and loved by this God who is so enormous. Nothing in your life can stop that from being true. No matter what you're facing, you'll only be able to make sense of it if you start by knowing how much he loves you."

Is there something I can hope for?

Something shifts within us when we start realizing just how big God really is and how much he cares for us. We start inviting him to show up in the middle of our circumstances, and we develop a deep internal conviction that he's going to come. We may not know exactly what he will do, or when he will do it. But he absolutely promises that he is with us,[26] and amazing things tend to happen when we partner with him in our everyday lives.

Wherever your story is taking you, I don't believe you've gotten to the end until God shows up and does something absolutely incredible, either with you, in you, through you, or for you. Sometimes we see it here on earth. Other times, we won't see the full picture until we stand with the Lord in eternity. But I fully believe that it's always, always true.

In the meantime, he has some gift planned for each of us every single day. Maybe it's wisdom or insight, or the ability to appreciate the small wonders of our everyday lives. But some days, it's going to be a miracle that takes our breath away. Knowing that, we become people of hope.

"So, what does all this mean? If God has determined to stand with us, tell me, who then could ever stand against us? ...Even in times of trouble we have a joyful confidence, knowing that our pressures will develop in us patient endurance. And patient endurance will refine our character, and proven character leads us back to hope. And this hope is not a disappointing fantasy, because we can now experience the endless love of God cascading into our hearts through the Holy Spirit who lives in us!" (Romans 8:31, 5:3-5, TPT)

God promises that he's going to be with us, no matter what. When we learn that it's really true, we start opening our hearts to the possibility of experiencing his goodness. It's hard to beat down people who hope like that. They just keep bouncing back up! Must frustrate the devil to no end.

> *When we ask God if there's still something we can hope for,*
> *He says: Yes, absolutely!*

> *Stop depending on your will, your resources, and your abilities.*
> *Come partner with me, and lean on mine instead.*[27]

A word to friends and family

The plain truth is that we all need each other, and we're stronger together than we are apart. Many times, the worst thing that happens to a person in crisis is feeling like they've become invisible. People avoid talking to them because they don't know what to say; but it isn't really all that complicated.

If you care about someone who's facing a long-term crisis, ask how they're doing and be willing to listen while they tell you. Don't be too quick to explain, correct, or "fix" them. Simply tell them you're sorry it's tough, and tell them what they mean to you. Remind them of the things that are still true, and the things that you like about them. Come to see them and bring a meal— or bring a movie and popcorn. Take their kids for the afternoon. Find a way that they can still do something they love, and a way they can contribute to the world, because we all need to feel valuable. Laugh together, groan together, cry together. Just *be* together. You don't have to be their sole support, but you can be a support.

When we all pitch in to help each other like that, it's amazing how strong we are. That person may remember your kindness forever... and the day may come when THEY are the ones helping YOU to thrive in a really tough place.

The rest of the story

What about Ian? He kept going, kept putting one foot in front of another, and kept turning to the Lord. The people in his church rallied around to help as he stepped into his new, single life. Several years later, he met and married Stefanie, whose own story is quite remarkable. They're very happy together, but they both want you to know that their finding one another wasn't the first miracle. They each say that first miracle happened long before they met. It was the way that God changed both of them from the inside out, and the real contentment and comfort and happiness they found in his presence, even in the middle of their struggles.

Stefanie says, "There's nothing that God won't carry you through. Nothing! No time that he won't stay alongside you. When you're in the pit of despair he will pick you up. And it will transform you in a way that wouldn't have happened if you just saw it in someone else. It's the most amazing, incredible thing. That's what I would wish for other people, that they could experience this kind of intimacy with God."*

The moment when everything changes

Whatever situation we're facing, the Lord has the answers that we need. He is our rescuer, our redeemer, our healer. What's going to happen when we stop clinging to our own pain and bitterness and self-will, and we start relying on him instead? Well, honey, that's when all bets are off, because his divine might and explosive power are working on our behalf.

"I've seen what you're seeing," he says. "Now why don't you come up here and sit with me for a while? It's time for you to see what I'm seeing."

That's when everything changes.

The flashes of his presence start to come, and we absolutely know that we are...Loved. Valued. Forgiven. Strengthened. Encouraged. "I know everything that's happened to you," he says. "All the scheming of the enemy. All the weight of your own foolish choices. All the terrible mistakes of others. All the brokenness of a fallen world.

"Be at peace. I am here. None of it, none of it, can ever separate you from my love."

---

* You can find Ian's story on page 251 and Stefanie's story on page 256.

And suddenly, we start to laugh because we know it's true, and we are filled with joy.

Recap: God Isn't Mad At Me

God is still good, even when life feels bad. He isn't mad at us. Instead, his heart is for us, and he's crazy in love with us!

We may all love the mountaintop experiences in life, but we don't have to be afraid of the valleys. They're often the places where we grow the most, where we find out who God truly is and who he is for us. Whatever challenges we face, he promises that we won't go through them alone. He will be right there—with us, in us, and for us—and that changes everything. When we learn how to remain in his presence, even in the tough places, that's when our greatest challenges start to become our grandest adventures.

After that... well... who knows what wonderful things could happen next?

Connection: The Snake In The Garden

God began Creation with his eyes wide open.
He knew that we would fail. He knew he'd have to redeem us.
Could it have happened like this?

"There's a snake in the Garden," the Father reported. "It's Lucifer. He was hiding, but I saw him."

The Holy Spirit shook his head. "We knew that he would come. Adam and Eve are so happy. They're whole and unbroken. Linked to us. Linked to joy! We've invested them with free will and built them to carry glory. Lucifer will find that offensive. He'll see it as an affront, and it's certainly one that he's going to answer."

The Father nodded. "Yes," he agreed. "But I would have loved having a little more time with them before everything happened."

"Sooner or later," he continued, "they're going to fall. Lucifer won't play fair. He'll watch them and wait for a weak moment. Then he'll spring a trap. It's the huge risk we've taken, giving them freedom of choice. But I don't regret the gift! I love them for who they are, and I love who they're going to become."

Jesus shifted position. He looked distant for a moment and his face tightened, as if he were seeing something very difficult ahead. Then he looked up and his face cleared. "I'm ready," he said with grim determination. "When the time comes, I'll redeem them. I understand the cost and I'm prepared to pay it."

The Father looked at Jesus with concern, and then he spoke soberly. "When they fall, we'll have to turn them out of the Garden for their own protection. If they eat from the Tree of Life after that, they'll be trapped in a fallen state. It can't be allowed to happen! I want so much more for them."

"Then we'll prepare another Garden, and another Tree," Jesus answered. "Gethsemane... and the Cross! They'll call that 'The Tree of Death,' but it's going to bring them an entirely new kind of life."

The Holy Spirit, too, looked at Jesus for a long moment, his eyes filled with concern. Then he laughed. "Lucifer won't ever see it coming!" he said. "He can't understand love, so he won't understand sacrifice. He'll play right into our hand. He'll steal the lesser gift. He'll never realize that he's making room for something so much greater."

"Speaking of love," the Father said, "I'm on my way. I'm going to spend a little more time in the Garden, loving on my son and my daughter. They're going to need it. There are tough enough times ahead for all of us. The Plan is so big! They won't understand it at first. They'll need massive doses of our love. It will be what carries them through."

A price was paid to redeem you ... the precious blood of Christ... God determined to send Him before the world began.
1 Peter 1:18-20 (VOICE)

Chapter 4:

I Don't Have

To

Earn

His Love

*Laura*

Some people say that all religions teach us basically the same thing: "Do good, and good will come to you."

Even Christians who claim they believe in grace often really believe that.

Yet secretly, we worry: What if we're not good enough? Is God going to lean over the edge of a cloud and zap us with a fistful of lightning bolts?

Then comes Jesus.

He changes everything we understand about God...about good religion... and even about goodness itself. He turns our question inside out, giving us an answer that's so much better than we could have hoped for.

Can we ever do enough good to be good enough? I can't wait for you to find out!

Can we ever do enough good to be good enough?

I want you to meet my friend "Rachel." We're catching up with her for a quick coffee between appointments. Almost everybody who knows Rachel wants her insight and help with their situation because, when Rachel comes in, it's like pressing the "easy" button. Things around her just work better.

It's not because Rachel takes charge. Quite the opposite! She makes YOU feel competent and important. She's great at sorting things out, so that your natural gifts and strengths feel like the very thing we need most of all, right here and right now. And if you look like you need to dial it down and take the day off—or even leave something undone altogether—Rachel will encourage you to do that in a way that leaves you feeling like a total success instead of a total failure.

But Rachel says things weren't always like that for her.

"My life used to revolve around all my activities," she says. "It started innocently enough. I thought doing all those things for God showed him how much I loved him. If I did more, I thought it would please him more. And then maybe I would feel better about myself.

"But it never feels like you're doing enough. There's always one more thing you need to do. And you keep trying, but you get worn out. Eventually you give up. I thought I'd never do enough to please God. That's when I started having real problems. I turned into a control freak and nobody even wanted to be around me. You think you're free when you're in charge of everything, but that kind of life isn't freedom, it's slavery."

A lot of us have lived like Rachel did. We tell ourselves that doing LOTS of good things shows God how much we love him.

> *But that's not what's really going on, is it?*
> *And is that actually what God wants from us, anyway?*

Desperately trying to be good

Let's get real here. If you're going crazy and wearing yourself out, either trying to "be good" or to "do good," it's possible that deep down, you don't really feel that you ARE good—at least, not good enough—to earn God's love.

> *Check yourself out. You'll know if it's true.*

Love and significance, and I mean *the real thing*. We all need it. We may feel like we don't have it. We may even think that we don't deserve it. But we fervently hope that maybe, just maybe, if we try hard enough, we can earn it.

Have you ever hoped that by doing enough good, you could be "good enough?" That's about like Cinderella thinking that, if she just empties one more trash can, her life will be different and she can finally sit down to a nice dinner with her stepsisters. The trash cans aren't the problem; the whole system is broken. Good luck with that one, girl.

Cinderella needs an intervention, and so do the rest of us. We've nearly all tried it—thinking we can earn God's affection by doing enough good deeds for him. And good deeds are great! But that whole "makes-me-better" plan just doesn't seem to work like we think it should.

Then there's this other guy I know. For a while it looked like "Mick" was trying to go down in flames, doing things he shouldn't be doing. Because of that, he thought God wasn't even interested in talking to him. But actually, he was dealing with the flip side of the same problem. He was buying into the same lie—that all God wants is for us to do enough good, so that we can be "good enough."

How does it really work?

Goodness defined

I used to think of "goodness" as people doing what we're supposed to do and being nice to each other. But the life of Jesus completely redefined goodness for us, and he literally meant it when he said, "Only God is truly good."[28] If you really want to get this, now, you might have to stop thinking of "goodness" as an abstract idea. Instead, think of it as a *tangible spiritual substance*. It carries weight and impacts its surroundings. True goodness is part of the essence of God. It's what comes out of him, because it's what's within him. It oozes out of every pore of his being and fills the air of heaven with his fragrance.

It's sort of like this. Imagine spending time in an apple orchard on a sunny fall day. Fresh green leaves and brightly colored fruits surround you. You breathe deep, smelling the scent of warm apples. You can touch them. You can taste them. If you squeeze them, out comes apple juice. You can even smoke their flavor into meats by burning apple wood. All of those are tangible expressions of the nature of an apple tree.

In much the same way, goodness and joy, truth and love are tangible expressions of the nature, or essence, of God. (You can learn more about his nature in Galatians 5:22-23.) But make no mistake! When love, joy, and peace are human-sourced, they're only pale imitations of the real thing. When they come from God, they're entirely different: empowered, supercharged, and brimming with *life*.

True goodness only comes from God. It's much more than an attitude or an action. It's an actual substance that brings *life* everywhere it goes. When we encounter true goodness, it's like we suddenly catch a breath of the air of heaven. We see things differently; we want to do things differently. We're refreshed, renewed, recharged, and repurposed.

Goodness lost

There was a time, in the beginning, when Earth knew the goodness of God. His feet walked it onto our soil. He breathed it into our air. His hands touched the hands of men and women. And God's creations, Adam and Eve, were literally made to be connected with his goodness. They knew God, heart-to-heart and face-to-face. The river of his goodness, his power, and his *life* would have been flowing through them all the time.

That's what Adam and Eve lost when they were tempted by Satan and fell.[29] They stopped relying on God. Then they tried bringing their own version, "human goodness," to the table instead. Only that didn't work, because our human goodness is just a cheap imitation of the real thing. God's goodness actually brings *life*, while the best we can hope for is being nice to each other.

The depth of that loss must have been truly staggering for them. Did they feel the ache of longing after the presence of God was gone? Did their hearts remember what it felt like to be touched by glory?

Time passed. One generation followed another—men and women who had never felt the touch of God's presence quite like that. And we forgot what had once been; we thought it was only an old story. But our hearts remembered. We longed for something we had never felt. Our hearts still yearned for that missing piece.

> *Without an actual link to the heart of God, though,*
> *his life would never flow through us again.*

Searching for the "missing link"

Our hearts truly were made to be connected to the heart of God. We all keep searching for that missing piece, even if we don't know what it is that we're looking for. Then we experience what I call the "goodness gap." It's the distance people feel between their hearts and God's. We try to bridge the "goodness gap" by doing enough good, to be good enough, so that his approval and his life can flow through us again. Only, as Rachel says, it feels like we can't ever get there. There's always one more thing to do.

"I'm a pretty good person." "I think I'm good enough." "At least I'm a better person than *she* is." We keep defending ourselves, trying to bridge the goodness gap with our words as well as our deeds.

Back in Bible times, the Pharisees[30] thought they had it all figured out. "We can do this!" they told each other. "If we just keep the Ten Commandments, really well and all the time, we can bridge the gap." So that's what they did, all day, every day. They even created rules around the rules, so they could be sure they were keeping the rules.[31] What an exhausting way to live! Once they got that going, it looks like they taught it to everyone else. And let's give them credit. The Pharisees rocked the rules. Nobody ever did it better.

But what they were selling? Jesus wasn't buying it.

Why we can't ever be good enough

In what we call the "Sermon on the Mount," Jesus takes the stuffing right out of the Pharisees. *Think you can bridge the goodness gap by keeping the rules? Well, just try THIS, guys.* Jesus says: "You're familiar with the command... 'Do not murder.' I'm telling you that anyone who is so much as angry with a brother or sister is guilty of murder." (Matthew 5:21-22, MSG)

Well, that was a pretty pointed comment.
It's obvious that the Pharisees were basically famous for being angry.

Jesus goes on and on like that. He uses the very law the Pharisees thought they knew (and owned). Only Jesus wields it like a surgical scalpel, laying their hearts bare and exposing the ugly darkness that lurked within them. *Ouch!*

What would you have said if you'd been there? I know what I'd say. "Jesus, it's impossible! Nobody can ever be that good, all the time."

And I think he would have grinned.
At last, you're getting it.

The Apostle Paul was a former Pharisee who finally caught on. Here's how he explains it: "Now do you see it? No one can ever be made right in God's sight by doing what the law commands. For the more we know of God's laws, the clearer it becomes that we aren't obeying them; his laws serve only to make us see that we are sinners." (Romans 3:20, TLB)

BAM! There we go. *That's actually the point of the law—it shows us that we, ourselves, literally can't keep it.* Here's all of humanity, and I mean everyone since Adam, saying, "I can bridge the gap. I can be good enough." Then there's the law. I think it's God's way of asking us, "How's that working out for you?" It's sort of like giving an EKG to a very sick man. It can't fix him. But it can show him that he's in heart failure, and he needs to seek help.

The law is like that. It shows us that we truly can't bridge the goodness gap. On our own, we'll never do enough good to be good enough.

The only one who is truly good

We can't afford to be stuck thinking like the Pharisees did—that we can bridge the goodness gap by really working at it. Seriously, give it up, guys! Jesus already showed us that our plan was impossible.

But he didn't stop there. Next he showed us God's way, by doing the impossible. After all those centuries of spiritual drought and longing, God's actual goodness walked the earth once again, in the person of Jesus Christ. What he carried was so much more than human goodness. Jesus showed us what true goodness looked like when he healed the sick, raised the dead, restored the outcasts, and just generally made things right.[32] He could live like that, because he was linked heart-to-heart with God the Father.[33] There was no gap, for Jesus. God's goodness flowed through him like a river of living water, constantly bringing life, real life, to him and to the world around him.

In that same sermon where Jesus takes all the stuffing out of the Pharisees, he says something else that's so significant. When I first saw this, I was so shocked that I couldn't take it in.

"Do not think that I came to *abolish* the Torah or the Neviim [the Law or the Prophets]. I did not come to *abolish* but to *complete*." (Matthew 5:17, OJB)

> *Hang on. Can we run that one by again?*
> *Jesus did not come to abolish, or do away with, the Law.*
> *Instead he came to complete, satisfy, and fulfill it.*

Here's what Jesus means. He's using actual, legal terminology. He's talking about the law of Moses like it's a contract. We all knew that, right? But in fact, it's a very specific kind of contract. Not a forever contract; *Jesus is saying that Moses' law is a performance bond.* It has been sitting around, unfulfilled, for centuries. Nobody has ever met its conditions. Nobody has ever been qualified to fulfill it.

At least, not yet.
And now? Jesus says that's exactly what he's going to do.

It's a bit like the moment when Babe Ruth supposedly pointed to a spot in Chicago's outfield, and then hit a home run exactly there. Only the fence Jesus is pointing to isn't a mere 440 feet away. It's so far off that it's just a dark smudge on the horizon. Remember those "impossible" standards he threw out at us? The ones where you're not only behaving right, but the deepest parts of your heart are right, as well? The standards we could never, ever keep. Well, Jesus says that's exactly what he's going to do! That's how he's going to "fulfill" or complete the law.

How about that? When God gave Moses the law, all those thousands of years ago, he was actually putting something in place that only Jesus could fulfill... *because he already knew that Jesus was coming to fulfill it.* If our hearts were longing for God, I get the feeling that he was longing for us, as well. He was setting things up so that he could bring us the answer.

God is always surprising us like that! He left all kinds of clues laying around in plain sight. You can see them all through the Old Testament, once you realize what you're looking for. But if you're not looking, you'll miss them. His plan was so big that only someone who knew his heart could have seen it coming.

Satisfying God's performance bond

Jesus uses legal terminology again when, with his last earthly breath, he shouts, *"Tetelestai!"* [34]

"It is finished!"

That's the formal word an official would stamp onto your mortgage or contract to show that it had been "Paid In Full." Once, that paper would have had a lot of power over you. It would've had so much power, in fact, that you could go to jail if you didn't keep its terms. But once it's marked "Paid In Full," it's only an old piece of paper. All its power to hurt you has been done away with.

That's exactly what Jesus did for us. He completely fulfilled and satisfied our debt to God, so it could be marked "Paid in Full." He's the only one who could ever do enough good to be good enough.

Do you see it? Maybe, like Rachel and me, you used to think that the law was an impossible standard, put in place by an impossible God. But that's not true at all! He's not an impossible God. Instead, he's the God of the Impossible. He paid our debt in full, doing for us what we couldn't ever do for ourselves. And he did it all...for love.

Jesus bridges the gap

Now you can see why Jesus told his disciples at the Last Supper, "This cup is the new covenant in my blood." [35] He was authorized to make a NEW covenant with them, because he was fulfilling (or completing) the OLD one. Once we trust in Jesus, that old contract, the law, is done away with. It did its job. It showed us that we couldn't ever do enough good to be good enough.[36] Now, though, we actually connect with God in a completely different way. It's the new covenant that Jesus himself made with God on our behalf.

Under the terms of this new covenant, we stop relying on our puny human goodness. Instead, we rely on Jesus' goodness, which is obviously way better.[37]

Jesus, you see, is the One who's right with God. And keeping this "new covenant" with God is all on him. As long as God is okay with Jesus, and Jesus is okay with us, our connection to God is secure. Listen to this:

"Since we've compiled this long and sorry record as sinners ...and proved that we are utterly incapable of living the glorious lives God wills for us, God did it for us. Out of sheer generosity he put us in right standing with himself. A pure gift. He got us out of the mess we're in and restored us to where he always wanted us to be. And he did it by means of Jesus Christ...Having faith in him sets us in the clear...[and] makes it possible for us to live in his rightness."
(Romans 3:23-26, MSG)

> *Couldn't you just eat that up?*
> *God's sheer generosity. His pure gift.*
> *When we trust him, he sets us in the clear.*
> *That's how it's possible for us to live in his rightness.*

If you've been exhausting yourself trying to earn God's love, that's enough to change your life, right there. We don't have to earn his love. He already loves us! We just have to stick close to Jesus.

Coming back to the river

Thinking about the law used to make me feel ashamed... yes, ashamed, that I wasn't a better person. Now, instead, it fills me with joy and wonder, because it so completely shows off what a super-hero Jesus really is. When I think about all that he did for us, I'm speechless. He's the only one who ever could have bridged our "goodness gap."

Seen from that point of view, isn't it funny? The very idea that we could earn God's love by being "good enough" ourselves! If we think that, we're giving ourselves far too much credit and we're giving God far too little. Compared to Jesus, we'd all look like a bunch of low-wattage light bulbs going toe-to-toe with a Supernova.

> *Can we ever do enough good to be good enough?*
> *That's exactly what Jesus already did for us.*
> *Could we ever earn God's love?*
> *He already loves us more than we can possibly imagine.*

Now for the "why." I hope you're sitting down.

God wants to touch the earth with his goodness again, starting right where we are. Jesus paid the full price so that, just like him, we too can once again be connected heart-to-heart with Father God. He opened the channel, so the river of God's goodness can flow into us... and fill us up... and then start flowing out of us. That's so much more, and so much better, than simply being nice to each other. We're talking about experiencing *real love* and *real life*, flowing our way from the presence of God. It's exactly what Jesus promised: "Rivers of living water will brim and spill out of the depths of anyone who believes in me." (John 7:37-38, MSG)

How is that possible? It only happens when the source of life, for us, is something much bigger than our own human spirit or will.

The rest of the story

How does that affect our lives? Well, just look at Rachel. I suspect her "old" brand of goodness tended to leave people feeling like they had just been run over. But now it's different. Her friendship makes the rest of us feel valued, refreshed, lifted up and empowered. The grace she carries just brings out the best in the people around her.* And then there's Mick. Remember him? His whole life is changing, and his family's life is changing as well, because he actually got connected to God's amazing love.

Now, you see, the pressure is off. We're not "doing good things" in order to be loved. Instead, real, genuine goodness starts flowing out of us, simply because of the way that we are loved.

The river of God's goodness is flowing again. It's time for us to stop clogging it up and blocking it off with our fear and doubt and unbelief. It's time for us to trade in our puny human goodness and trade up to God's kind. Let's accept his amazing gift, purchased at an enormous cost so he could give it to us as a massive inheritance. This is too precious and too important to miss. And there's a thirsty world out there, dying for a drink of God's living water.

---

* You can find Rachel's story on page 261.

77

Dream with me for a minute.
Imagine that river flowing out through all believers, everywhere.

What do you suppose would happen then?
I don't know. But I'd sure love to find out!

Recap: I don't have to earn his love

Can we ever do enough good to be good enough?

It's foolish to try; our puny human goodness couldn't ever "earn" God's love. It's actually just a weak imitation of his goodness, anyway. But God's got it covered! When we trust in Jesus, he digs a deep channel so that the life-giving river of God's true goodness starts flowing into us—and through us—and then out of us.

Now for the best news of all:

We don't have to earn God's love. He loves us already!

Connection: Watching From The Sidelines

Don't you realize that I could ask my heavenly Father for angels
to come at any time to deliver me?
Jesus in Gethsemane, Matthew 26:53 (TPT)

The Archangel Michael steeled his nerves and steadied his hands as they gripped his sword. Tears ran freely down his face as he stood his ground. His own pain was nearly more than he could bear, and he turned his eyes away from the terrible sight of his Master, nailed hand and foot to the roughened Cross.

What the humans saw was bad enough: a man, nearly unrecognizable because he'd been beaten to a pulp. Blood streamed down his face from the crown of thorns, set in place to mock his kingship. He had to push up against the nails again and again as he strained to draw each breath. But for most of them, the sight, mercifully, was limited to the pure physical brutality. Few of them were fully awake, so they could not see the true horror that was evident to every spirit being who was present on that hill:

God Himself had taken on the sins of the world.

Deceit, betrayal, rejection, murder, and every other evil thing lay heaped upon Jesus' back. The One who was the very Author of Life had chosen to make himself subject to death. It truly was inconceivable.

Then Michael saw the slightest movement in his ranks, and he was alarmed. The Plan was clear. There could be no deviation.

Living in the YES!

"Hold!" he cried. His voice cracked with the strain, so he cleared his throat and belted it out in the unmistakable voice of command.

"HOLD!"

The demons misunderstood, and their jeers and catcalls increased. "That's right!" one whined. "Just try to hold the line! But it's too late. You can't stop it now. He's going to die!"

Michael flashed a warning glance at his commanders. Each gave him a barely perceptible nod; they understood his meaning well enough.

Hold back.
Don't interfere. It's the Father's Plan for Jesus to die.

Michael fully trusted the Father.

It was the hardest thing he'd had ever had to do. Everything within him strained to step in and defend Jesus. His tears ran unchecked as he steeled his nerves again, and he steadied his hands as they gripped his sword.

It was by God's grace that [Jesus] experienced death's bitterness on behalf of everyone…this is how he brings many sons and daughters to share in his glory.
Hebrews 2:9-10 (TPT)

Connection: Storming The Gates Of Hell

We're not clear on everything that happened between Jesus' crucifixion and resurrection. But we're told that, had the devil understood God's plan, he never would have crucified Jesus. Might it have looked like this?

"Is it finally finished?" the devil wondered aloud.

The reports from Earth had been troubling him for years. Jesus just kept on fixing things that had looked like they were well and truly broken. Then, as if that wasn't bad enough, he started sending out disciples who were doing pretty much the same things he did. "We're losing control of the earth," Lucifer had fretted. "Who knows where this is going to end? I have to put a stop to it somehow."

But now he finally thinks he's got everything under control.
God can't fix things this time, because Jesus is dead.
And yet...can't shake that feeling...Has he thought of everything?

Suddenly alarms start blaring all over the place. Aides are running in from every direction, screaming their heads off, bringing damage reports. All of Hell actually has broken loose.

WHAT? They are saying that HE is here—not dead, but very much alive! How is that possible?

BOOM! BOOM! BOOM! BOOM! BOOM! The awful concussion pounds the air, again and again, as an unimaginable force assails his inner fortress. Lucifer cries out and shields his eyes as blinding light splits the gloom, coruscating with its brilliance.

He squints against the light and sees that it seems to be emanating from the figure of a man. Yet, as Lucifer knows all too well, this Being is far more than just a man. He is resplendent, glorious, armed for battle and utterly terrifying. His voice throbs and pulses with pure power, so that it sounds like rushing waters. As he speaks, the very essence of Hell itself writhes, withers, and curls away from him.

He answers Lucifer's question with finality.
"Yes," he declares in a voice like thunder. "It is finished."

Then the devil shrinks back as Jesus reaches the Gates of Death and starts tearing them off their hinges.

"I have come for my people," he says.
"Their debt has been fully paid. You cannot hold them any longer."

Much later, the devil sits with his back to those awful, wrecked gates, surveying the chaos around him with a rising sense of despair. He hadn't seen this coming. He'd completely underestimated the love of God.

Meanwhile, all of Heaven is going wild with celebration as Jesus returns. Radiant glory streams from his presence as thousands of angels shout with unbounded joy. A massive column of people follows him in through the gates. Most of them look a bit dazed; they all look incredibly happy. He has done it! Jesus rescued them from death. Now he's bringing them back to be with him forever.

Then he placed his right hand on me and said: "Do not be afraid. I am the First and the Last. I am the Living One; I was dead, and now look, I am alive for ever and ever! And I hold the keys of death and Hades. Revelation 1:17-18 (NIV)[38]

Chapter 5:

He
Welcomes Me
Into
His Family

 *Laura*

Let's just be honest here.

Some people are quick to say that God is good. But secretly, they either feel distant from him... or else they keep him at a distance. Maybe they aren't quite sure how God feels about them. Or maybe they've been told that he's only looking for obedient servants, people who will blindly follow his rules and do his bidding without asking too many questions.

Other people act like they're part of God's family. Yes, they come to him with respect; but they're also expecting love and connection and intimacy. It's a different kind of relationship.

Which is true?
Is God calling you to be a family servant?
Or is he inviting you to be a family member?

Does God see you as a family servant or a family member?

"I was adopted from Russia when I was twelve," Ellen remembers. "It was exciting, but everything was very different. The food was different, the culture was different. I didn't speak any English. I had to see a lot of doctors and dentists and tutors. I missed Russian food, and the culture and the language, and I missed my old friends. Before, I'd been living in an orphanage. Now I had a new country, a new language, and a new set of parents.

"My new family said that they loved me. But really trusting them? That took me a long time. You know, letting them in and letting them care for me, I wasn't sure about that."

As Ellen remembers the ups and downs of her early years in America, sometimes you want to laugh out loud and sometimes you want to cry. There were funny misadventures, like that first Christmas when the whole family almost missed having their pictures made. (They'd spent *several hours* arguing about whether Ellen had to wear red-and-green like everyone else, when she wanted to wear pink-

and-purple.) There were also wrenching moments when everyone ended up sad and hurt.

Keeping her distance

It was easy for Ellen to learn "about" her new family—where they worked, how they lived, and what they did with their time. But although she "knew about" them, she didn't really *know them*. She didn't know what they loved or hated, what they dreamed of, or who they truly were. Also, as someone like Ellen would understand all too well, you don't really know someone until you see what they're like when everything goes sideways.

It was easier, at first, to keep her distance.

It was easier to assume that her new family would end up being like other people she'd known—people who had hurt her and let her down. Coming from that perspective, it was easy for her to misunderstand and misinterpret the things they said or did. Then she'd become hurt and suspicious all over again. Needing to feel safe, she did what any wounded person might do: she held back. She kept high emotional walls guarding her heart, and she defended them fiercely.

Sadly, those high walls didn't actually keep Ellen safe. Instead, they just kept her locked in with that awful loneliness and pain. Only after many years was she ready to tear down her inner walls and really let her new family into her heart. It can be tough for older adopted kids to find that kind of courage. I'm so glad she did!

Ellen's story is very personal for me, because she is my much-loved daughter. When we were living through those painful years, it felt so frustrating. I kept thinking: *Why does this have to be so hard? Can't she just realize that we're good people who want to be good to her?* But now, thinking about things from her point of view, it's easy to see why, for Ellen, love and trust would have been really scary.

Sometimes love and trust can be scary for all of us. Have you ever been in a similar situation, where you spent time with someone, but you couldn't really relax around them? Did you first have to make sure that it was safe, and that you truly belonged?

Keeping our own distance

In a way, Ellen's story is relevant to all of us. Here's why: Sometimes we all do the same kind of thing with God.

Do we hold our relationship with God at arm's length, or hold back a part of ourselves? It's easy to settle for simply knowing "about" God. We can stop at believing what others have said about him, instead of experiencing a deeply personal connection for ourselves.

Maybe we've been told that God is big. But like Ellen in those early years, we aren't quite sure about things. We wonder: Is he really that good? Will he be good to us?

Perhaps we think God is distant, and he's much too busy running the universe to bother with our little problems. Maybe we've been told that he's harsh, judgmental, and angry, or we're afraid that he's disappointed in us. Or we worry that getting close to God will leave us looking weak and feeling vulnerable. Maybe we just think that life is already good enough. Why mess with success?

We have no idea what we're missing.

Being adopted into God's family

Just as our family adopted Ellen, God says that he wants to adopt each of us into his forever family. Listen to this:

"And you did not receive the 'spirit of religious duty,' leading you back into the fear of never being good enough. But you have received the 'Spirit of Full Acceptance,' enfolding you into the family of God. And you will never feel orphaned, for as he rises up within us, our spirits join him in saying the words of tender affection, 'Beloved Father!' For the Holy Spirit makes God's fatherhood real to us as he whispers into our innermost being, 'You are God's beloved child!'" (Romans 8:15-16, TPT)

I am God's beloved child.

What wonderful words! For anyone who has wondered how God feels about them, that's the bottom line. *I matter to him. He loves me!* It's what adopted children like Ellen need to hear, over and over. In fact, it's what all of us need to hear. God invites each of us into relationship, into intimacy, into something that's real and secure and lasting.

I am God's beloved child.

Tragically, in some parts of the world adopted children are treated like family servants instead of becoming family members. But Paul was thinking about Roman culture when he wrote those verses. For the Romans (and for us), adopted children and biological children were treated alike. They received the same affection, the same protection, and the same full rights of inheritance. They shared in the family's fortunes and privileges, and they were involved in reaching for the family's interests and goals. Adoption conveyed a permanent sense of, "You're one of us! You belong here." And that's God's invitation to each of us. It's a vast, immeasurable gift, and an immensely powerful promise.

You are my beloved child.

Pause for a moment. Imagine God wrapping you up in his arms and whispering those words, over and over again. Feel the connection, the commitment, the love.

That's the kind of relationship God is offering to each of us. But like Ellen, each of us has to decide how we're going to respond.

Becoming beloved children

"You are my beloved child."
What does that really mean?

It means that you're not just "one of the crowd." God doesn't just want us to "behave well" and not be a bother to him. He isn't interested in turning us into shiny, fake, cookie-cutter "nice people" with no real originality. He doesn't want us to lose our sense of self, and he doesn't swallow us up in his big personality. Instead, each of us is unique, and we are uniquely special to him.

God sees each of us as an original, and his love for us is intensely personal.[39] Yes, he sees what we say and do; but then he looks much deeper. He looks past the things we do to fill our time. He looks past the pain and disappointment that hold us back, past the awful mistakes we've made. He looks beyond the shallow identities we cling to, as if they could make us feel important. He sees our true selves—he sees us as we were meant to be—and he calls us by name and he loves us.[40]

> *You are my beloved child.*
> *You are my beloved!*

The Lord welcomes us into a place where we feel valued, but not because of our human accomplishments or moral striving. Instead, he's inviting us to just come on in and be loved. He tells us that *we matter*, simply because we matter to him.[41] That's such good news, because he never changes.

The Bible says that God knows us intimately and loves us passionately.[42] He knows the best things about us and the worst things about us, and he still loves us! [43] He isn't lonely, so it's not like he "needs" us. It's much better than that; his love for every one of us is intentional. He says that we matter to him. He *chooses* to value us. He *chooses* to love each one of us, and he chooses to spend time with us.[44] And he invites us to come into a place that, on our own, we wouldn't dare to go.

You see, the awesome, powerful, majestic Ruler of the Universe offers to share something with us that's far more than just what he wants us to "do" for him. He makes us far more than mere servants, doing his bidding because it's our religious duty.

Instead, he makes us his beloved children. He offers to reveal Himself as he truly is, and he offers to share his heart.[45]

In the process, we learn what it's like to really feel loved.

"Knowing about" or really knowing

As we spend time with the Lord, an interesting thing happens: we become changed. It's not exactly that we're trying harder. But being loved like that transforms us from the inside out.

Here's the thing. God invites us to *actually experience* his presence. In that place, like the disciples on the road to Emmaus, we find that our hearts are strangely warmed.[46] When we pray, we discover that he answers back, as we hear his still, small voice whispering to our hearts. We feel his comfort and joy. We see the words of the Bible leap off the page as if they have come alive, like a longed-for letter from home, bringing us wisdom, strength, laughter, and insight. And we find that worship isn't merely our "performing" for God. Instead, it's a precious, stolen moment of intimacy with the One who knows us best and loves us most.

As we spend time with the Lord, the Lord spends time with us. He whispers words of encouragement into our hearts. He touches us with his love, and he gives us good gifts—real treasures like hope, help and healing. He does things for us that we can't do for ourselves.

He gently loosens our grip on the hurtful things we often cling to, things like fear, unbridled anger, bitterness and unforgiveness. Instead he gives us much better gifts, like genuine love, deep peace, and real freedom in our hearts. Along the way, he helps us to become who we were always meant to be: whole, real, authentic people, fully connected to him and to each other. People who live with a sense of purpose and find joy, even in the middle of hard times.

All of that happens when we truly know the Lord.
It's just what being in a relationship with him is like.

Becoming part of the family

Over time, the Lord begins writing his love and his nature into our hearts. He brings us to the place where we can run to him without fear, no matter what happens, because we know that **we are his.**[47] Whether you're just beginning this journey, or you've been drawing close to God for a long time, he's inviting you to come closer and discover more of his great heart for you.

We are his beloved children.

Knowing "about" God may inspire us. But *truly knowing him* fills us with a sense of wonder, and life with him is just way better. He actually wants more for us than we want for ourselves—more hope, more joy, more strength, more healing, more love. That's what life is like in his family. Let's not settle for the spiritual equivalent of living alone and in poverty, while he's throwing open the door to the mansion and inviting us to move in.

The rest of the story

What about Ellen? Over time, she was able to push past her fears and draw close to us. I'm so glad she did—glad that I get to know this warm, wise, funny, strong, resilient, amazing person. Here's what she says:

"I moved away from home. I may have thought I had left my family behind, but God kept coming after me. He kept saying, 'Come, come.' Then he gave me the time I needed, till I was ready. Till it was *my* decision to say, 'Okay, Jesus, I'm going to follow you.'

"Now I know—once, I *was* an orphan. A lot of bad things *did* happen. But that's all in the past, and I don't have that feeling anymore. I belong to this family. I think it's what God wants for all of us. Wherever we are, he sees us. We can know that we belong to his family, that he loves us and he's going to stand by us, no matter what." *

Ellen has her own family now, and many of the things she likes best about us are being carried forward into the next generation. Other things, like our quirks and silly habits and foibles? We all laugh about them together. Everyone says it's easy to see the genuine affection we all have for each other. It's interesting how much we now have in common, too—many of our ways of thinking, our values, even our facial expressions and mannerisms. We've rubbed off on Ellen, and she's rubbed off on us.

Maybe that's the sort of thing the Apostle Paul meant when he said, "So all of us ...can see and reflect the glory of the Lord. And the Lord—who is the Spirit—makes us more and more like him as we are changed into his glorious image." (2 Corinthians 3:18, NLT)

God's nature rubs off on us. He loves us, grows us, and transforms us.

God's sons and daughters

God is looking for people like that: sons and daughters who spend time in his presence, reflect his image, and know his heart.

---

* You can find Ellen's story on Page 264.

Living in the YES!

Really getting to know him? Becoming more like the One who floods us
with abundant life and brings real hope into every situation? I'm in!

What about you? Don't settle for merely knowing "about" God, when truly knowing him is so much better.

I am not God's beloved servant.
I am his beloved child.

One day, God says he's going to have a huge banquet in heaven. [48] It's going to be the mother of all parties. He's setting your place at the table. I hope to see you there!

Until then, he's inviting you to come on in to hang out with him, every single day. He'll celebrate with you in the good moments, comfort you in the bad times, help you to see things from his perspective, and generally make every day better.

Everyone needs a Father like God.
Are you ready to let him father you?

Recap: Welcome to the family!

God isn't just looking for servants who will blindly do his bidding. Instead, he's inviting each of us to become part of his forever family. He's inviting us to *know him*, deeply and intimately, like much-loved children drawing near to their beloved Father. And as we actually spend time in his presence, it just seems like his nature starts to rub off on us.

Come closer and feel his wild, tender love for you. Feel God wrapping you up in his arms right now and whispering, "I love you! You are my beloved child."

Connection: Storming The Gates Of Heaven

What really happens when we pray?

Imagine that you're a brand-new, baby Christian. A friend told you that you could enter God's presence boldly in prayer. You're not quite sure about that, but they said it's a big deal. Apparently Jesus paid quite a lot to make it possible. So now, here you are, creeping towards the gates of heaven. *What should you do next?*

You gasp in awe as the splendor of the gates takes your breath away. People dressed in lovely clothes stream in and out. Going in, some of them look sad and weighed down, while others seem relaxed and happy, even excited. You do notice that nobody who's leaving seems quite as sad as the incoming faces. In fact, some of them are *actually glowing.*

> *Those must be saints! you think.*
> *That's not for me. I wouldn't belong.*

Finally, you spy a much smaller entrance on the side, marked "Servants." Of course, it's still far bigger and much grander than anything you've ever seen on Earth. *That's it! That's what you'll do.*

So you pause for a while, collecting all your courage, and then you make a run for it. As you get closer, you slow down, dreading what will happen if they catch you and turn you away. But maybe, you think, maybe if you keep your head down, you can slip in with the crowd and at least catch a glimpse of what it's like inside.

Your heart pounds as you draw nearer. This just might work.

But NOTHING is getting past that gatekeeper. "STOP!" he commands in ringing tones, and suddenly your feet seem to be frozen in place.

Everyone turns and looks at you
as the gatekeeper strides purposefully in your direction.

"Oh, no!" you wail inside. "This is it. I've been caught! What a stupid idea. What was I thinking? Why did I ever come?"

Then the gatekeeper breaks into a huge smile. "This is the Angels' Entrance," he explains gently. "All of us need to log in, report on what's happening, and get our new orders. Family members always go in at the big gate, so we can give you a proper welcome. See? It's over there! Come with me. I'd love to show you the way."

Let us then approach God's throne of grace with confidence, so that we may receive mercy and find grace to help us in our time of need. Hebrews 4:16 (NIV)

Connection: Hiding In The Halls

Which do you think are most important: the things you take to God?
Or the things you bring back from your time with him?

Okay, now. You take a deep breath. You're going to try this again.

You're determined to come boldly to God's presence in prayer. So, first, you get dressed up in your finest clothes. Then you grab your best good deeds and stuff them into a bag. You plan on laying them at God's feet with a flourish.

"Family entrance... family entrance," you mutter to yourself as you timidly draw near the gates.

But then you get to the actual halls of Heaven. Surrounded by glory, you start to feel dingier and dingier. And your best good deeds? You look down and realize with horror that you're only carrying an old pillowcase full of dirty rocks. That's when you find a little nook in a back hall. You slide down to sit on the floor, as you wonder what you should do. Hours later, you're still sitting right there, feeling horrible and trying not to cry. That's where Jesus finds you. He kneels down beside you, but you can't meet his gaze. You just feel so ashamed.

"Look at me," he says firmly.

As Jesus looks into your eyes, you know that he sees *everything*. But you don't feel judgment coming from him, only kindness. "You don't have enough goodness, do you?" he murmurs. "That's okay. I have plenty. Let me give you some of mine."

He takes hold of your hands, and a sort of life-giving warmth begins flooding into you and filling your whole being. All fear melts away as you look into his eyes, and a sense of pure *love* begins bubbling up.

Then Jesus grins broadly, his eyes twinkling with merriment. He gestures vaguely at your pillowcase. "Next time you come, don't worry about bringing that old stuff," he says lightly. "We don't have a cover charge here, you know. It's more of a come-as-you-are kind of place. Just come!"

You look up at the splendor all around you. Then you look down at your grimy little sack. You don't feel ashamed anymore, though. It just strikes you as terribly funny. You're not sure who starts chuckling first, but it hits you both. His joy is so contagious! Soon you're both laying flat-out on the floor, belly-laughing.

"I need to introduce you to the Holy Spirit," Jesus finally says, wiping tears of laughter out of the corners of his eyes. "He takes care of everybody who comes around. He packs the best swag bags[49] and party favors you've ever seen. No matter what you have when you come, nobody ever needs to leave here empty-handed!"

Continue to grow and increase in God's grace and intimacy with our Lord and Savior, Jesus Christ.   2 Peter 3:18 (TPT)

Chapter 6:

I Am

Really

Forgiven

Laura

Forgiveness is freedom! It means blessed relief from guilt, pain, and shame. And we all need it. For the times when our best efforts aren't good enough... and for the times when we don't even try to bring our best.

Some people try to deal with their faults and failings by minimizing: " It really wasn't that bad." Others just live in torment. And tragically, sometimes our mistakes can't ever be fixed. We can be left to wonder:

Will I be defined by my mistakes and shortcomings forever?

As we look deeper into this important subject, we're going to find that the bad news is much worse than we thought.

But there's also good news.
And the good news is much, much better than we would have dared to dream.

Will I be defined by my mistakes and shortcomings forever?

Dream with me for a minute.

Imagine gathering up every single burden and shame and regret you've ever carried, every what-if and every if-only. Then think how it would feel if you could just roll them all up into one great big ball and throw them away.

"If only it were that simple," most people say.

But the Bible says that's what God's forgiveness actually means.

Listen to Vijay's story. It's all about forgiveness and redemption, and how God's answer is so much bigger and better than we ever could have imagined.

"I was addicted to porn," he begins.

"I was a Christian, right? But I couldn't wait to finish my prayer time to see that stuff. Now, I'm so glad to be free! The guilt and shame, they really tear you apart. It's like you've got a backpack full of concrete blocks, and you're carrying it all day long. It feels so heavy."

You can read more of Vijay's story in the back of the book, as he unpacks for us what drove him to do the things he did. * And his story has it all. He was deeply hurt by others, and he hurt others deeply. There's intentional wrong, inflicted on purpose in order to cause pain. There's harm people didn't mean to cause (but did), and even harm that happened when they meant to "do good" (but didn't). There are small hurts and big hurts, and all of them did hurt. You can glimpse the whole tangle of the tragedy as it spills across from one generation to the next, and then starts all over again. Sin is just a mess like that, and whether we want to admit it or not, our own sin always, always hurts someone. We all really need forgiveness.

The problem is worse than we thought

My husband Bob explains it like this. Our granddaughter's adorable little teddy bear lives at our house. But what if Teddy got dropped into a great big vat of used motor oil? You could fish him out. You could squeeze him out. But try as you might, you could never really wash him out. Even if, by some miracle, you could clean his plush fur, he would just stain himself again and again—and probably get you dirty as well—because his whole stuffing would be soiled from the inside. It would never really come clean.

That's the picture the Bible paints of "original sin," and the problem is much, much worse than we thought. You see, our "sin" is far more

---

* You can find Vijay's story on Page 270.

than just a long list of our misdeeds. Instead, if we're not connected to Jesus, we're all a lot like Teddy: created to be wonderful, but impossibly ruined from the inside. Much like Teddy's stuffing, the Bible says that our insides—our will, our thoughts and intentions, all the way down to our spirits—are just sort of messed up. Sometimes we'll all think and do and say things that are just going to come out wrong. [50]

Much like Teddy, we can try to clean up the outer layers of our lives. But it doesn't really work too well, does it? Maybe we can control our language or our actions, at least temporarily (and while other people are looking.) Still, one way or another, the dark stain on our souls just keeps leaking out. From a human point of view, some of us may look cleaner than others. But remember, we see people from the outside in. God sees us from the inside out. From that point of view, we were all hopelessly stained, soiled, and unrepairable. And that's another thing about Vijay's story, by the way: quite honestly, some of the worst harm was inflicted by supposedly "good," religious people. ALL of us need God's grace.

Now, if a teddy bear had been dropped into used motor oil, we would probably just throw it away. And some of us would actually do that with another person—decide they were past redemption.

But not God.
He loves each of us way too much for that.

Discovering God's amazing answer

What are we going to do about a problem that's so big we can't fix it?

Think about everything we've explored so far: God's magnificent splendor. His burning holiness. His amazing love. His heart, on fire with passion for his people. How he's like a loving Father caring for his children. How he isn't mad at us, and how he wants to help us, not harm us. How he sent the law, like an EKG, to show us that we were in spiritual heart failure and needed help. How he sent Jesus to put skin on and pay the full price for every sin we would ever commit. Most of all, remember the powerful lifeblood of Jesus, eternally crying out from God's Mercy Seat and declaring his amazing grace.

God understood our problem far better than we did. And he created a solution that was so sweeping in scope, so magnificent and vast, that it takes our breath away. Actually, his answer is so big that we struggle to take it in. You see, God doesn't just give us really good soap, so we can work super hard to clean up the outside of our lives, again and again. Instead, from the moment we trust in Jesus, something truly amazing happens:

> *God completely remakes us from the inside out...*
> *so that our spirits actually aren't soiled anymore.*

Listen to this wonderful montage of Scripture:

"Your sins have been permanently removed because of the power of his name...God still loved us with such great love. He is so rich in compassion and mercy. Even when we were dead and doomed in our many sins, he united us into the very life of Christ and saved us by his wonderful grace! ... Now, if anyone is enfolded into Christ, he has become an entirely new creation. All that is related to the old order has vanished. Behold, everything is fresh and new ... God made the

only one who did not know sin [that's Jesus] to become sin for us, so that we who did not know righteousness might become the righteousness of God through our union with him."
(1 John 2:12, Ephesians 2:4-5, 2 Corinthians 5:17, 21, TPT)

Are you trusting in Jesus?
Then the Bible says that your sins have been permanently removed.
Their former power over you has been broken.
You have become an entirely new creation!
Dear friends, that is the meaning of God's wonderful forgiveness.

God is serious about forgiveness

Forgiveness is such a big deal to God. It's time for us to understand the massive nuclear power blast that happened when Jesus died for our sins and then rose again in his eternal form.

You see, he didn't just "calm" or "soothe" or "ease" our sin problem. Instead, he blew it to kingdom come! If you are in Christ, you ARE a completely new creation.[51] From God's point of view, these are the facts:

- He has given you a new heart.[52]
- He has breathed onto your spirit. It isn't dead anymore; it's alive.[53]
- You're now clean, stain-free, and deeply connected to God![54]

If you're a Christ-follower, God actually doesn't call you a "sinner." Instead, he calls you a "holy one." [55] Sure, you may have a sin habit that you'll need to deal with. You may have old, destructive patterns of thinking that you'll have to fight to overcome. But, dear friend, *none* of that is more powerful than the Blood of Jesus.[56]

See, I think we get it all wrong. When we feel stuck or broken, we keep telling God that our sin problem is really big. God, on the other hand, keeps telling us how his forgiveness is much bigger. It's time for us to step into the amazing, powerful spiritual reality that he bought for us. It cost him so much. Don't you dare let it go to waste. God isn't focusing on your sin! He's focused on getting you set free. He wants you living in his grace.[57]

Standing in the waterfall of grace

How does this forgiveness thing work? Let's check it out.

This passage comes from 1 John 1:7-9 and 2:12 (TPT). We're going to break it up and talk our way through these verses.

"If we keep living in the pure light that surrounds [the Lord,] we share unbroken fellowship." *Did you catch that? It's possible for us to have unbroken fellowship with God! That's what this is really all about.*

Here's how it happens:

"The blood of Jesus, his Son, continually cleanses us from all sin." *Yes, you heard that right; look it up in the Greek. Jesus' blood cleanses us from all sin, continuously! He didn't just fix our problem halfway. What he did is the real deal.*

"If we boast that we have no sin, we're only fooling ourselves." *What if you don't think you have a sin problem? In other words, you may be saying something like, "I'm a pretty good person. I don't really need to be forgiven." Then God is basically saying, "You're kidding, right?"*

"But if we freely admit our sins when his light uncovers them, he will be faithful to forgive us every time. God is just to forgive us our sins because of Christ, and he will continue to cleanse us from all unrighteousness."

Now, you've really got to take in this next part. But maybe you'd better sit down first, because it could come as a bit of a shock.

"Your sins have been forgiven on account of his name."

Yes, you heard that right. It's written in past tense. It has already been done! **You have been forgiven** *because of Jesus. He really did it all!*

Have you ever told God, "I'm a pretty good person?" Or are you more of the "I'm so horrible that he'll never be able to love me" type? Either way, in this passage, John says that you should stop kidding yourself and simply come to God just as you are, mess and all.

You can pray something like this: "God, I can't do this on my own. My goodness isn't ever going to be enough. Will you accept Jesus' sacrifice to pay for my sins? I want to be connected to you."

And God says, "YES."

Once you do that, John says it's like you're standing under a waterfall of grace. Grace washes you continuously. And seriously, God is doing the heavy lifting here; the Greek verbs are very clear about that. You're just doing the receiving.

What's your part? You stick close to Jesus. You stay in relationship with him. If you realize you've done something wrong, of course you're going to come to him and say, "Lord, I'm so sorry." But don't come to him out of fear! Come to him out of love, with a willingness to change. We just make choices like that for the people and the relationships that we really value.

Are we offended by the Gospel?

Does that whole system seem wild to you? It did to me at first.

Growing up, I'd heard some crazy stuff. I thought God was very angry and sin-focused, so I thought I'd better be sin-focused, too. I thought that God turned his back on me every time I had unconfessed sin in my life. As a result, I was constantly whipping out a huge magnifying glass, gazing at my own navel to hunt for unconfessed sin. When I first heard about God's continual forgiveness, I was actually offended. "That can't be right!" I argued. I went hunting in the Bible so I could prove my point... and found out that I couldn't. To this day, the more carefully I study this, the more clearly I see the truth. *Our sin was a much bigger problem than we knew. But God's forgiveness is far better, and waaay more powerful, than we ever dreamed.*

Today, I realize that the old lie didn't even make much sense. It would be really hard to be in relationship with another person who shut me out every single time I made a mistake. *On again, off again? Are we speaking to each other today, or not? What do we think God is, bipolar?* We'd be apologizing constantly, unsure of ourselves, and miserable. We'd be treating Jesus as if his enormous sacrifice, his lifeblood, meant nothing at all. It's ridiculous!

If you've been living like that, it's time to take the pressure off. Drink in these wonderful words of reassurance: "Blessed are those whose transgressions are forgiven, whose sins are covered. Blessed is the one whose sin the Lord will never count against them." (Romans 4:7-8, NIV) God is so much better and kinder than any of us. He makes this wonderful truth crystal clear in Scripture over and over again, because he wants us to feel secure in his love. I think it's time we started believing what he actually said, don't you?

We are really, truly, completely forgiven.
Standing under the waterfall of his grace.
This news is so good, it's hard to take it in.
Only God could have dreamed this up!

This is the face of grace

What happens when people actually start living like this?

Well, I'll tell you what doesn't happen. I've never seen anyone discover the waterfall of God's grace, and I mean *actually experience* the wonder of it all, and then go out and try to get as dirty as possible. Instead, we get really excited. We feel valuable. We feel loved. And the response is that we love God back, even more. Old problems that we thought had us trapped start fading away. We may need to get help from a pastor, a counselor, or others. We may have to work at things. But it's not a chore anymore; it's an adventure.

Let's get back to Vijay. He told me that when his story started, he would've described himself as a very hard, tough guy. But then he told me about the first time he *actually encountered* the tangible presence of God. "I cried my eyes out," he said. "It felt like that moment was just for me. I had told others many, many times that God is our 'Abba' Daddy, but that was the first time I experienced what it really felt like. That was something else. From there, a full inner healing process began. It was very intense. It was after that, that I got set free."

111

"Before," he goes on, "it was terrible. Really, you're living your life in bondage. The day I finally felt forgiven, I didn't know I could live like that! I didn't know I could smile like that. I'm not even a sinner anymore, because all my sins have been forgiven. Now I can look at myself in the mirror and say, "I'm an awesome child of God.""

During our interview, Vijay told me that some of the most "religious" people he knew had a hard time forgiving him, even after it was clear that he had changed. I think that is so sad.

As I look at the footprint of his life today, it blows me away. God's grace and kindness just roll off of Vijay. His wife and kids have shiny eyes as they talk about him, and he's one of the most encouraging guys you'll ever meet. He's totally transparent about the areas where he's struggling to grow right now, and he is going for the gold. He's 100% sure that every one of God's answers will make his life even better.

> *I look at Vijay and think about who he was.*
> *Then I think about who he is now.*
> *And I think: that's what forgiveness is all about.*
> *This is the face of grace!*

Becoming fruitful

Once you really link up with this next bit, you just might start getting happy. You see, it's about the "why."

Why did God go to that much trouble and expense to secure real forgiveness and true freedom for us? What happens when we start living this way? Jesus gave us a clue when he told his followers, "I am the vine and you are the branches."[58] Let's check it out, so we can understand exactly what Jesus was talking about. *Imagine we're standing in a vineyard.*

Now, here's the thing about vines: if their leaves are clean, if they get enough water and they have good strong sap coming up from their roots, then you just add sunlight and magic happens. *Voila!* They produce wonderful fruit. It's the most natural thing in the world for them.

But let's imagine that our vintner is walking through his vineyard one day. He notices that some of his precious vines are trailing on the ground, and their leaves are getting muddy. He shakes his head and says to himself, "No, no, no. That will never do." He knows that muddy vines don't do well, because the mud keeps them from drinking in the sunlight. If you leave them like that, they'll start to wither. If you leave them like that long enough, they may even start to die.

So what happens next? Well, our vintner certainly doesn't attack his precious vines with a weed whacker! Instead, he gently lifts them up. The more withered they've become, the gentler he is. He washes off the mud so that the leaves can take in sunlight again. Then he lifts them up and ties them to a good strong frame, so they can stay out of the mud and stay clean. Once he does that, they green up, start growing, and eventually start making grapes again.

That's such a great picture of what forgiveness really means. It's a whole system, and Jesus invites us to live in it. Are you connected to the vine, so that you're drawing life from God? If so, that's wonderful! If not, ask him to graft you in. Once you're connected to him, let him wash the mud off of your life and set you out in the sunlight.

"I am a true sprouting vine, and the farmer who tends the vine is my Father. He cares for the branches connected to me by lifting and propping up the fruitless branches and pruning [or, literally, cleansing][59] every fruitful branch to yield a greater harvest. The words I have spoken over you have already cleansed you. So you must remain in life-union with me, for I remain in life-union with you. For as a branch severed from the vine will not bear fruit, so your life will be fruitless unless you live your life intimately joined to mine... You must continually let my love nourish your hearts." (John 15:1-5, 9, TPT)

> *Your love, continually nourishing our hearts.*
> *Jesus, there's nothing we want more!*

So... if a healthy grapevine produces grapes, what fruit do we Christians produce when we're truly, deeply connected to the Lord?

It generally looks something like this: Things about us start to change. We feel loved. We become more joyful and peaceful, more grounded and even-tempered. We develop a resilient strength. In some ways we're able to take ourselves less seriously, because we feel more secure. At the same time, it seems like our lives take on greater significance. We start genuinely caring for one another. Check out the ways that God describes his own essential nature in Galatians 5:22-23. When we're connected to him, the "good fruit" in our lives is really just an expression of his essential nature, flowing into us and then flowing out through us—often, while we aren't even aware of it.

Connected and fruitful: it's an amazing kind of life. In fact, if you could get all of that happening, and I mean *really happening*, with a whole group of people, why, you'd have the Kingdom of God breaking out all over the place.

What does this mean for us?

All the life is in God.[60] He's made a way for us to get connected to his presence and then stay connected. We don't have to go away, wait till our "leaves" get dirty, and then come back to wash them under the tap. And it's no good living in the mud, either. Instead, come stand with Vijay and me under the waterfall of God's grace. Then watch as his *life* starts flowing through you.

It's time to let go of those old lies and sin habits; they aren't ever going to make us truly happy. But we'll never be sorry enough, disciplined enough, or good enough to deal with them by ourselves. We all need the Lord's massive, powerful forgiveness and his help.

Here's the key. God's forgiveness doesn't depend on our confessing the same sins over and over again, while we keep clinging to a deep sense of shame. Instead, our sins are forgiven, *really forgiven*, because they are under the blood of Jesus.[61] When we accept his sacrificial death on our behalf, God washes away all our sin from the inside out and makes us new.[62] It's time for us to finally accept that truth.

Because of what Jesus did, our past doesn't have to define our future.

From that point on, we can just live in his presence. When we need to deal with something, the Lord will let us know. Then we get to experience true repentance, which is really pretty awesome.

You see, true repentance doesn't mean living in perpetual, self-centered regret and misery. Instead, we're accepting God's invitation to transformation. We turn our hearts towards him.[63] As we do, we suddenly realize that we've been clinging to something that's dead and stinking and gross. *Ewww! Yuck!* We don't even want it anymore, so we open our hands. We let God take it away, and then he washes us clean.

Once we really get that, we stop hiding from our problems. As Vijay says, when you learn what it feels like not to have any rocks in your backpack, you don't want any more rocks. So you do what it takes to experience real freedom! That's certainly what God wants for you. Don't hesitate to get real help when you need it, from someone who knows how. Learn how to confess and believe hope: "Jesus is going to be Lord over my problem."

What if that isn't working for you? When someone is caught in a sin that they can't seem to overcome, they're often dealing with a broken heart or deep soul wounds, or else they're believing a lie. And God isn't throwing up his hands and saying, "You miserable thing! I can't believe you haven't taken care of this!" Instead, he's gently and firmly telling us, "That's hurting you, isn't it? Are you willing to let it go? I don't want it to obscure the glory that I put within you. Come up here with me. I have something much better to give you."

The Lord actually wants better, more abundant life for you than you want for yourself. And his ways make that possible! Let him wash the dirt off of your life. Bask in the sunlight of his love. I think vines must really enjoy being fruitful. And I think that you will, too.

Recap: I am really forgiven

We don't have to be defined by our mistakes and shortcomings anymore. The good news about God's forgiveness is real and true.

Isn't it wonderful? We're not grudgingly or partially forgiven. We're not poor beggars, hoping to stand in the back of Heaven's throne room one day, keeping our heads down and our mouths shut. Instead, because of Jesus, we are fully, completely, gloriously made new!

It's time to accept God's wonderful gift of real forgiveness, his gift of real life. It's time to embrace everything that means.

We are forgiven. We are free!

Connection: My Chains Are Gone

What awful weight do you carry? Is it guilt or regret? Something you said or did? Something you didn't do? Then this is for you...

You're walking up a steep hill. It's such a chore trudging along. You've been dragging that ball and chain for so long. Everyone else you see has one, too. It's just the way of things.

Then someone comes up alongside you, striding easily and whistling cheerfully. He slows his pace to stay in step. Why do things seem so easy for him? That's when you notice:

He doesn't have a ball and chain.

You resent that at first; it seems so unfair. But it's impossible to hold onto your resentment. Something about him just warms your heart.

"That looks heavy," he remarks, looking down at your leg. "It must hurt. Why are you carrying it?"

You sputter and spit for a while, and you fire off a short, angry answer. But then the whole, painful story comes spilling out as he listens intently.

"I'm so sorry," he says with genuine compassion. "Would you like to take it off?"

"Yes," you answer simply. So he kneels down and takes hold of the shackle with his bare hands. You hear a loud *crack* and feel a vast rush of relief as the hateful ankle bracelet falls away. Then you look down in astonishment and see it lying, shattered, on the ground. There's blood on the shards—not your blood, but his.

And now it's gone! It's not a part of you anymore!

You look down in wonder. You kick your leg experimentally. Then you start to run. You feel so light! Suddenly the sun isn't beating down on your back, it's simply shining warmly on your face. You run for a few minutes in sheer delight before you realize something is missing. Then you trot back to rejoin your companion. It's just nicer traveling together with him.

"Thank you!" you exclaim. In the depths of his eyes you see compassion, joy, understanding, and love.

He looks back at you as if he really sees you. "You're welcome," he answers with a warm smile.

Everyone who believes in him is set free from sin and guilt.
Acts 13:39 (TPT)

Connection: Not Guilty!

Imagine being in the greatest courtroom of all—Heaven's Throne Room. You're the prisoner standing in the dock. Your Accuser, the Devil, rises and clears his throat. Then he reads out a very long list of charges against you. Your breath catches and your stomach sinks. Oh, no! What are you going to do?

Jesus strides up. He turns to you, smiles reassuringly, and whispers, "It's okay. I've got this." Turning to the Court, he declares, "I am this client's defense attorney. Let me see that list. ... Oh, yes, that sin. I remember it. I paid for it. Hmm, this one...Yes, I paid for this one, too."

Jesus is silent for a long moment as he looks up and down the list. Then he looks the Accuser full in the face. "As a matter of fact," he says bluntly, "I paid the full price for every sin you have listed here."

Jesus touches the list with his nail-scarred hand. You look on in pure amazement as every accusation vanishes. He holds up the paper, showing you—and everyone else—that it's now only a clean, blank, empty page. Then he brings it forward and confidently hands it to God the Father.

"Very well!" Father God remarks. "All of this seems to be fully resolved." He looks sharply at the Accuser. "Do you have any other charges?"

Quaking with fear, the Devil mutely shakes his head. He knows that no accusation he brings can stand up to the Blood of Jesus.

The gavel comes down decisively. BAM!
The echo of it rings through the courtroom.

"Then this defendant is declared NOT GUILTY! He is cleared of all charges. Bailiff, remove those chains. Case dismissed!"

You turn to Jesus, laughing and crying at the same time, and give him a huge, grateful bear hug. He hugs you back for a long moment. Then he holds you at arms' length and looks at you with genuine affection. "That old Accuser may try to bring up that list again," he says to you with a grin. "If he does, you let me know. And tell him that you won't be talking to him anymore unless your Attorney is present!"

That's when the Holy Spirit comes up, grinning broadly, and joins in. He gives Jesus a fist bump and then turns to you. "Let's celebrate!" he laughs. "Then there are a few things we're going to do together. We're going to have some fun!"

This gracious gift leaves us free … acquitted with the words "Not guilty!"   Romans 5:16 (TPT)

Chapter 7:

He Has

Given Me

His

Righteousness

Laura

What is righteousness, anyway?

When something is "righteous" or "rightways," that means it isn't bent, broken, twisted or warped. Instead, it's been put to rights so that it's real, true, sound, well and whole. All in all, it's functioning as it was meant to be.

That's what we all need, isn't it? Being made whole, so we can function fully, as our true selves. That's what righteousness does for us. It's one of God's greatest gifts, and experiencing it flat-out changes your life.

I can't wait to show you how!

Discover the joy of living as your true self!

Tula says, "The night of my high school graduation party, my boyfriend got into a fight. By dawn, he'd been charged with murder. It was like a living nightmare, and the shame was almost unbearable. One day I was drawing pictures of wedding dresses, and the next day I was thinking about ways I could kill myself. I'd worked so hard to have this perfect image—the perfect Christian, the straight A student— so nobody would look too closely and see how broken I actually was on the inside. Now it was like the covers had been pulled back, and everybody could see that it was all a lie.

"I felt desperate. My future hardly seemed like it was worth living for, but it turns out that God had other plans."

If you'd met Tula prior to this point in her life, you would have thought she had it all together. She was an achiever. She was smart, friendly, ambitious and attractive, always involved in whatever was going on. On the surface it looked like she had everything going for her, but that wasn't the whole story. The abuse she'd survived as a child had contaminated her inner world with a toxic mix of fear, pain, and shame.

She'd been valiantly trying to contain it, but now she had sprung a leak, and now her very existence was threatened.

What about you? Maybe you're like Tula. You know that you're broken; you know that you need help. Or maybe right now you're thinking, "Nope. Nuh-uh. Not me. Life is really good, thanks." In either case, I think her story speaks to all of us. No matter how good a life you're living, this much is still true:

You were made for more.

There is a "more," purposed in the heart of God, and it's calling out to you. He designed you to live a life that most of us have hardly dared to dream about. We're usually not even playing in the right ballpark. How can we? We don't have a clue, and we're stumbling around in the dark ...at least until we truly understand what it is that we were meant to be.

Understanding God's original design

God made men and women "in his image." [64] That means he made us to be far more than mere physical beings. We were created to be *living spirits*, his much-loved sons and daughters, deeply and intimately connected to him. What would that really have been like?

You hear God's steps in the garden and your pace quickens. Your heart leaps as you think: HE'S HERE! God's face lights up as he sees you, and you throw yourself at him with complete abandon. Wherever he is, that's your favorite place. You lose track of time as his boundless love, perfect wisdom and pure joy flood into your being.

"I can't wait to tell you what happened today," you laugh. Then the two of you lean your heads together as you tell him what's going on. You're facing a challenge, but you're not afraid. There's a great purpose for your life, and he has made sure that you're well-equipped to accomplish it. Any time you're uncertain about something, you know that you can just ask him. Sometimes he tells you what he thinks. More often, he asks you questions. You've learned that searching for the answers either changes the way you see things...or else it changes you. One way or another, though, he always helps you to find a solution.

You love the life you live. You're fearless and real and totally transparent. You have no sense of shame. Instead, you're filled with pleasure at God's absolute acceptance, love and delight in you. You've learned that he is powerful, wise, loving, kind, hopeful, joyful, able... and the more you spend time with him, the more you're becoming like him. The life that flows through him also flows through you. Even the trees in the garden seem to turn greener and grow faster when he's there. Now they're beginning to respond to you in the same way. You're starting to wonder: just as he's teaching you how to tend and cultivate the Earth, so that it becomes fully alive, is he tending and cultivating you?

But that's a question for another day. For now, it's time to laugh together, cry together, just BE together, with the One who knows you best and loves you most.

That's what Adam and Eve would have experienced before they fell. It's what they (and we) were made for. Pure *life* coursed through them continually, like a river flowing straight from God's presence.

We become dead men walking

When the devil tricked Adam and Eve into cutting themselves off from God, though, that river of life would have dried up instantly. It was still there; but by their own choice, it wasn't there for them. Life as they had known it—*real life, true life, constantly flooding into them from the inside out*—was gone for good. They became mere shadows of the glorious beings they once had been. And the dim half-life that was left to them? That was all they had left to pass on to us.[65]

From that point on we've all been incomplete, left to cope with pain, shame and brokenness. With some people, it's obvious. Others, like Tula, cover it over with the appearance of success. But it affects us all; and the worst news is the living death.

Imagine having a vase full of cut flowers. They may look good. They may even smell good, for now. You may love the way they brighten the room. But if they've been cut off from their roots, they're actually already dying from the inside out. You'll know that for sure in a few days when you lift them out of the water, smell the putrid, rotting stems, and wail, "Eww! Yuck!" as you throw them away.

Every one of us is basically like that. If we're not connected to God, so that his *life* is flooding through us, we're really just dead men walking. We've been cut off from the true source of real life. We're only poor shadows of the glorious beings we were originally meant to be.[66]

God's daring plan

That's where we were. Our spirits were irreversibly dead and broken. We couldn't fix ourselves any more than our poor cut flowers could reattach their severed roots to their own slimy stems. *But God could, and he did.* His wild love for us demanded a response to our pain. He wasn't going to leave us like that.[67]

That's why God himself, robed in limitless glory and power, shrouded in majesty and mystery, stepped out of eternity and into time. It's why he laid aside his God-nature, put on human flesh and became a man.[68]

Everywhere he went, Jesus reversed the symptoms of our living death. You could tell where he'd been because he left behind a great, shining trail of *life*. He healed the sick, restored outcasts, and just generally made things right. And that was only the beginning! At the Cross he willingly absorbed all of our brokenness and sin, took our fallen condition into his own body, and died in our place.[69] He entered hell and beat the devil on his own turf.[70] He forcibly took back all that had been stolen from Adam and rose from the dead in his glorious, eternal form.[71] All of Heaven must have gone wild with celebration as he returned there in victory.

Next came the moment when all of Heaven held its breath.
It was the moment they'd all been waiting for.
Maybe it went something like this...

Jesus solemnly entered Heaven's Most Holy Place. He'd been dreaming of this moment for millennia, and he smiled as he came to stand before the Great Altar. In his mind's eye, he saw the faces of all those he loved. (He saw your face.) Then he set to work cleansing the Altar. Using his own life's blood, he completely obliterated the awful stain that had been left there by mankind's betrayal. He had done it! He had secured our complete redemption. He'd altered the very fabric of reality, so that now he could actually reverse our "irreversible" condition of living death.[72]

"For God made the only one who did not know sin to become sin for us, so that we who did not know righteousness might become the righteousness of God through our union with him"
(2 Corinthians 5:21, TPT)

Jesus bought the right to put you to rights.[73]

It was an impossibly daring plan; and he did it all for you. He paid a price that was far greater than we've dared to imagine, and he secured a prize that is far grander than we've dared to dream. He saw YOU... really, truly healed and whole. Not just "pretending" to be okay, while your heart was actually broken and writhing in pain, but fully restored; and fully functioning out of a place of deep intimacy with God.[74]

Jesus saw the river of *life*, the river that flows from the Father's presence, flowing through you.[75] Everything that Adam had lost...Jesus bought it all back.[76] Now you can be fully connected to him,[77] so that you become real, true, sound, well, and whole. You can experience his true, wonderful, life-giving righteousness. Jesus restored the possibility of the Father's original design coming to life, in you.

Catch even a glimpse of everything God did for you, and you'll fall to your knees, speechless and awestruck. A love like that—and gifts like that—demand a response.

Ditching our pseudo-righteousness
(It's not that great a loss)

Do you want to activate God's gift?
There's something you'll have to do first:
You have to let go of your personal sense of self-righteousness.

Think about a time when you did a good deed, or made an important decision, and ended up feeling just a little bit superior to everybody else. (If that's never happened to you, you're welcome to borrow one of mine.) We're all pretty good at finding little ways to generate self-worth and self-importance, aren't we? They make for a pretty poor, cheap imitation of true righteousness; but we tend to cling to those things, when we think that they're all that we have.

Then we get just a taste of the true, powerful, life-giving glory of God.

And once we discover the real thing, we see our silly, self-generated pseudo-righteousness for what it is: nothing more than a cheap imitation.

Think you can make yourself righteous? It's about like taking those poor, wilting, cut flowers, spray-painting their withered petals with bright, cheerful colors, and hoping nobody will notice... that they're still dead.

If you want to change that situation, here's what you do: stop counting on your own good deeds to make you right with God. Lay down your personal, religious, and moral superiority. Just drop 'em all in the dust and don't even look back. Reach out instead to the One who is life itself, who is grace.[78] His gifts are so much better! He's

131

offering you his gift of true, living righteousness. That's what we were made for.

Experiencing real life

Let's check in on those poor cut flowers one last time. By now they're clearly dead. They're brown, withered, and stinky. And it's obvious that the bright spray paint was a terrible idea, because they really do look ridiculous. As we're watching, one more pitiful, bedraggled petal comes loose and gently drifts down to the tabletop.

But then God does something for them that we could never do. He cuts off the slimy stems and reconnects their withered shoots to his powerful roots. We watch in wonder as new life rushes in. That silly carnival-colored paint flakes off as they plump up and turn green. Fresh flower buds swell out, and new shoots start uncurling.

That couldn't really happen to a dead flower, of course, but it's exactly what happens to each of us when we stop relying on our own goodness and start relying on Jesus, instead. The Bible tells us, "Anyone who belongs to Christ has become a new person. The old life is gone; a new life has begun!" (2 Corinthians 5:17, NLT) And that is literally true. From that point on, everything about us starts changing.

What would it look like for you to live the same life you have now… except that it's God-breathed? What if his very life and nature start working their way through you from the inside out? If you can begin to imagine that, you may have just an inkling of what God really wants to do with you. It's a very different way to live, one that's only possible when we're connected to him. We get to collaborate with God!

Righteousness, Parts 1 & 2

Are you ready for righteousness? Part One is easy. It goes like this:

Jesus = Righteousness = Life. Period.

The moment you trust in Jesus, his *life* floods into you.[79] God forgives ALL your sins, puts your spirit to rights,[80] and reconnects you to himself. From that point on, you ARE forgiven, you ARE righteous, you ARE holy, and YOU CAN come into his presence without fear... not because of your good deeds, but because of what Jesus did for you.[81] You CAN turn to God and feel his love warming your heart.[82] You CAN listen to him and hear the whisper of his still small voice in your spirit.[83] *Reconnection and restoration:* that's what Jesus was buying when he paid such a terrible price. And he does all the heavy lifting. Really, all we can do is receive.

Then comes Part Two, "**All That God Gives Us.**" And, really, the Bible says God gives us so many things that I think "giving" must be one of his love languages! Check it out; he gives us:

- A new heart
- A new nature
- A new attitude
- New gifts
- New habits
- New character
- New perspective
- New values
- New expectations
- And that's just the beginning!

He really is the God who is "More Than Enough." [84] Anything, ANYTHING that's lacking inside of you, he means to fill that place.

Righteousness, Part 3 (the missing link)

When it comes to righteousness, though, this may be the most important part of all, and we often don't talk about it. For some of us, it may be the missing link in our walk of faith. What am I talking about?

The things God takes away.

Now, please don't get me wrong. I'm not saying that every loss we face comes from the hand of God. As we've already said, this world is a muddy place, spiritually, and many forces are at work here besides God's will. Some of the things that happen to us, we rebuke. Some we resist. And in my experience, God does a lot more "giving" than "taking away."

But sometimes he does "take away." If he does, you can be sure it's always because he's actually trying to bless you and protect you. [85]

Here's an example. Life can mark people with everything from small injuries to horrible traumas, and we deal with the mess in many different ways. We can all develop emotional scars, false identities, terrible relational habits, and poor coping mechanisms. Maybe you've ended up with a terrible temper. Or maybe it's fear, or shame, or depression, or a need to control everything.

Those things may feel familiar. You may even be proud of them. You may think they're a part of you; but what if they're not? There you are, protectively guarding a terrible attitude or a bad habit that you

134

may even treasure. But you keep finding yourself in uncomfortable situations. And God is right there, saying, "Oh, that's hurting you, isn't it? Are you ready to let it go?"

If you're like me, when that happens, you can find yourself snarling at the Lord. There you are, desperately clinging to your old attitude or habit while you say, "Oh no you don't! I need that." Meanwhile, he's asking, "Do you trust me? Look here; I have something so much better to give you."

You finally hand over your favorite "toy" with trembling fingers. That's when you find out that you were actually clinging to a lie. It wasn't really part of you at all.

Becoming David

God doesn't operate on some kind of cosmic layaway plan, where you say "yes" to him now on Earth, and then he waits... and waits... and waits...till he finally says "yes" to you in Heaven after you die. *Real life* is always flowing from his presence, and it starts coming to us here.[86] That's what Adam and Eve experienced before the Fall. It's how Jesus lived. More importantly, it's what he bought for you at a great cost. But it does help when we understand how the process works.

Imagine what it would feel like to be a huge, beautiful block of Carrara marble. You're the envy of all the other blocks, with your snow-white color and delicate veining. And yes, it doesn't hurt that you're mas-sively bigger than all the rest. You love showing off your personal splendor to everyone.

Then one day, WHAM! A whole chunk of you flies off in a shower of dust. "Wait," you cry out. "What's happening?" You cringe in horror as the chisel hurtles through you again and again with frightening speed. "Won't somebody stop this madness?" And hang on a minute, now... you needed that corner.

In those first moments and days, you have no idea what's going on. But over time, you feel a rough form emerging from your blocky shape, and you begin to feel less afraid. Now you have powerful arms and legs, and you feel such joy in their grace and symmetry. Where did they come from? You didn't know you had it in you.

Then comes the day when he carves your eyes... and you finally see the face of the Sculptor who's bringing you to life. You're actually there on the day when someone reverently asks him, "How did you carve the David?" and Michelangelo replies, "It was easy. I saw him within the marble, and then I took away everything else."

What is it like to become the David?[87]

God's dream for you

The David is a masterwork, and you are too. "We are God's masterpiece... the product of His hand, heaven's poetry etched on our lives." (Eph. 2:10, VOICE) But the Sculptor who's forming you works in a much more delicate medium than marble. He shapes the human spirit. In order to do that, he doesn't work so much *on* you as *with* you. He's adding, giving back and taking away until what's left is not only glorious and wonderful, but far more *alive* than you ever would have thought possible. When he gets to the end, you'll realize that everything he's taken away was *not-you*. You'll discover that he has truly formed the *real you*, and you'll be filled with joy.

136

That's what the Lord wants for you. Not a "broken" life, where you're barely surviving. Not a "fake" life, where you're smiling on the outside even though your heart is wounded and bleeding with pain. Not a "harsh" life, where you're taking out your hurts on everyone around you. But a *real life*, where you can be authentic, true, and transparent; where nothing is missing or lacking; where the vast reality of his *empowered* love, *empowered* peace and *empowered* joy can blast through you like a mighty river, because there's nothing blocking the flow.[88]

Interestingly, as we become more and more connected to God's presence, we become more and more like him. But we definitely don't become identical. We all have such different interests, and energy levels, and personalities, because God made us that way. Each of us is unique, because he has crafted each of us uniquely. And the Lord delights in that![89] He isn't interested in eradicating your personality. Instead, he means to eliminate the distractions and authenticate the real you. The more you're connected to him, the more you emerge from the shadows and come fully alive, until you actually become *your true, living self.* Here's what it looked like when that became real for Tula.

Meet Tula 2.0

"I'd lived all my life with so much pain," Tula admits. "I knew how to look like a success. I could make people think I was smart and even special, but nothing I did changed the awful rejection and shame I felt inside. When I looked in the mirror, I hated the person I saw. I thought I had to hide my real self from everyone, especially God. I'd been a Christian for years, but I'd never believed I was lovable, and I'd never felt his love.

137

"Then God came for me. And do you know what? He didn't come to my successes. Instead, he came to the ugliest, most broken places in my life to tell me how much he loved me, even then. That's when I began to experience his love for the first time. It happened when I realized: God wasn't pretending that I was something I wasn't. He didn't have to look at me through the blood of Jesus, so that he could stand the sight of me. Instead, he saw ME, all of me, just as I was, and he truly loved me.

"That changed my life. I used to feel like I was two different people, the successful, public 'me' and the broken, private 'me.' But not anymore! I've stopped pretending that I'm perfect, and I've stopped hiding my flaws. Instead, I think I'm becoming the person God always intended for me to be. He accepts me right where I am, and because of that, I can accept myself. I don't have to sit across the table from somebody and wear a mask to hide my real self. I don't have to perform in order to win God's approval.

"He's given me a new kind of wholeness. Now, if I make a mistake, or if those old feelings get stirred up, I handle it differently. I know it's really just going to be another opportunity for me to come to God and grow.

"My work doesn't define my value anymore. From the moment when

I finally saw the way God looked at me, I knew: I have value, because I am loved." *

His dream for the world

Now we've come to the most important part of all: the why. There's a reason why all of this is so vitally important. We can't afford to keep relying on our foolish, self-generated pseudo-righteousness. We can't afford to keep clinging to the old lies, hurts, and bad habits that hobble us and tie us down. There's a reason why the Lord of life subjected himself to death to purchase the total package of your true righteousness and complete freedom.

You see, God means to fill the whole earth with his glory.
And he means to do it through people like you.[90]

We can't do that by trying really hard. Don't even go there! I'll probably fall off my chair laughing, and then you will, too. That sort of thing isn't possible if we're depending on human ability. It's only going to happen through people who are regenerated, blood-bought, sold-out lovers of Jesus, who know how to partner with him. We humans are not life-generators; we never were. But we're certainly wired to be life-carriers.

I'm thinking about Kayle, who rescues prostitutes off the streets. Todd, who goes into Supermax prisons. Mel, who feeds the homeless.

---

* You can find Tula's story on Page 275.

Then there's Jay, who prays for drug addicts in the park (they often get healed on the spot) and James, the hospice worker I know who ministers to the dying. (Sometimes they get healed, too.) And don't forget Tula, the Much-Loved Daughter. Now she knows that she doesn't have to "perform" in order to win her father's affection. She's just living a genuine, wonderful, joy-filled life, one that affects everyone around her. That kind of miracle is only possible because the old pain doesn't define her anymore.

None of those people could keep doing that stuff in their own strength. They'd burn out! Instead, they've learned how to come into the presence of God to be renewed. You can ask any of them. They'll tell you that *real life* is what happens when we drink living water, straight from the presence of God, and get supercharged. It all starts in that deep place of really knowing him and experiencing the peace, the fire, the absolute glory of his tangible presence. It's that sense of, *He knows me... and I'm getting to know him better*. Everything else in our lives works differently when it flows from that.

I love drinking God's living water! Have you tried it? I think you will, too.

> *You were made to be real, true, well and whole.*
> *Connected to the presence of God.*
> *Actually carrying his glory.*

> *What is the "more" that he has in store for you?*

Recap: He has given me his righteousness

Jesus bought the right to put us to rights.

That's what true righteousness is all about; it's the incredible joy of getting to live as your true self. God is inviting us to let go of the old, false things that used to give us a shallow sense of meaning, and turn to him instead. As we do, he truly brings our spirits to life and reconnects us to himself. That's what we were made for. He makes us real, true, well and whole, and empowers us to live a glorious, meaningful kind of life.

We were made to be deeply connected to God and to know him intimately. There's a constant stream of *life* flowing from his presence. As we spend time with him, we find that it can flow through us.

Connection: Robes Of Righteousness

New clothes. New shoes. New attitude.

Oh, wow! You've been called into Heaven for a visit. The Father wants to talk to you. So you're preparing to enter the Throne Room and meet the King of Kings and Lord of Lords. You think you're ready—at least, you've gotten dressed up in the very best that you have. You hope Jesus will be there. You can't wait to see him again and tell him what's been happening with that goodness he gave you. It's great stuff! You and the Holy Spirit have had some really cool adventures together.

Then Jesus comes into the waiting room. He's wearing his God-form today, rather than the human one, and he's dressed formally for Court. Nothing could have prepared you for that. Your jaw drops as his splendor takes your breath away, and every thought flees from your now-empty head.

Suddenly you look down and see that your "best" only looks like a filthy rag next to his radiant glory. Once again you feel ashamed, but Jesus is having none of that. "I know you haven't been to Court before," he says kindly. "I've brought you something to wear. This is yours! If you like it, you can take it home and wear it always."

He unfolds a shimmering white robe and you go off to try it on. It's quite unlike anything you've ever worn. It's so comfortable! It looks just like the one you've seen him wearing, and it still carries the warmth from his hands. Even more, it carries the same indefinable fragrance that entered the room when he did. When you put it on, you stand a little straighter.

Suddenly you feel wonderful.

As you come out of the dressing room, Jesus' face lights up. "It's perfect!" he exclaims. Then he grins purposefully. "Come over here," he instructs you. Then he takes you by the shoulders and turns you around. That's when you see yourself reflected in a beautiful full-length mirror. Jesus is standing next to you, sort of behind and a little to the side, so that you see him, too.

Without thinking, you blurt out, "I look just like you!" Then you turn red and add, "Well, maybe a little bit, anyway*." But you worry: will he be offended? Did you go too far?*

He knows what you're thinking. As always, he knows. He grins and laughs. "That's why I gave it to you," he says with a smile. "This robe has a special effect. It reveals the truth. It brings out who you really are. As you keep wearing it, in some ways you will look more and more like me. I hope you don't mind! At the same time, it will simply help you to look more and more like yourself, your true self. Do you like it?"

"More than anything in the world," you whisper as you turn this way and that, checking it out. *This truly is a priceless gift.*

Jesus starts turning towards the door, but he's still looking at you. "Are you ready?" he asks. "Let's go in together. Dad told me that he can't wait to see you."

I am filled with joy and my soul vibrates with exuberant hope...
for He...wrapped me with the robe of righteousness.
Isaiah 61:10 (VOICE)

Living in the YES!

Chapter 8:

I Can Live

Connected

To Him

 *Laura*

"You are the light of the world," Jesus told us. But every light needs a power source, and we're no exception. What about you—where do you get your power, your hope, and your energy?

A lot of people carry on like they think God is having a power shortage up in heaven, and he needs for us to lend him some of ours. (That's why they pray and go to church, right?) But it actually works the other way around!

God is utterly glorious and amazing, and we come to him because he recharges us. He sustains the universe. He has way more than enough power left over to light up all of us, and he's incredibly generous about giving it away. He wants to link us up with a kind of life that most of us haven't even begun to imagine. He's wired us for it, he's set it up, and he's already paid the bill.

We just have to get plugged in.

Come get plugged in to the power!

"Life changed for me," Melissa says, "one night when my daughter was very sick. She had severe food allergies. Vomiting, seizures, trips to the hospital. This time she was curled up on the bathroom floor in a fetal position screaming, 'Help me, Mommy!' It was absolutely horrific. I felt like I was going to die because I couldn't help my child, and I was desperate. I'd been asking, 'Where are you, God? Your Word says there's no sickness in heaven. You healed everybody in the Bible. Why is my child sick?'

"That night, the Lord told me exactly how to pray for her. When I did what he said, she stood up immediately and said, 'It's gone!' And it was. Since then she has been extremely healthy, no more problems. We have freedom. Praise God!

"Now a righteous anger rises up in me when I see that the Liar has done that to somebody else, and I'm constantly asking people, 'Can I pray for you?' I have seen God heal deaf ears, I've seen him heal broken bones. I have prayed so many times for kids on the soccer field who looked like they were on the way to the hospital, and seen God heal them right then and there. It just fills me with joy every time I see God do that. It's such a beautiful demonstration of who he is.

"I didn't start out like this," Melissa laughs. "Before the age of nineteen, I was a party girl. Then my best friend got saved, and I wanted what she had." *

Getting in on the secret

If we're honest, a lot of us feel like Melissa did... at the *start* of her story. We're trying to live in a way that pleases God. Some days it works, and we gloat: *"It just happened!"* But other days everything goes wrong and we can only groan: *"What just happened? Where's the abundant life that Jesus promised?"*

It seems like things were different for the early church. Just look at the people in the book of Acts. Whether they have good days or bad days, whether they're supported or persecuted, the results are the same. They draw even closer to God, pray for more boldness, and start seeing even bigger miracles. They live amazing lives; and they turn the world upside down. [91]

Every possible kind of Christian gets involved: men and women, young and old, rich and poor, black, white, and everything in between. There's only one kind of Christian we don't find in those early accounts, and that's a powerless Christian. *Every single one of*

---

* You can find Melissa's story on page 287.

them seems to have a special connection with God that changes their experience of life itself.

How do we get in on their secret?

The Museum of Modern Lighting

Imagine we're going to see the famous lamp collection in the Museum of Modern Lighting. (Don't go hunting for this particular place, though. I made it up.) As we drive up the hill, we gasp at its striking ultramodern architecture. We walk in, exclaiming over the brilliant white walls, whole banks of skylights, and acres of floor space. Then we start touring the collection. As we stroll through the galleries, we see every possible kind of lamp, from tiny dollhouse lights to enormous crystal chandeliers. Some of them are set on pedestals. Others are mounted on the walls or ceiling. But something is missing.

"Why aren't they turned on?" we wonder aloud.

The curator is mortified. "We don't believe in electricity," he declares stiffly. "We believe in natural light. That's why we invested millions of dollars in our state-of-the-art skylights. Aren't they beautiful? We think they really show off our lamp collection. But for the very best experience, we do recommend that you wait for a sunny day, and then come between the hours of ten and two. That's when the daylight is strongest, and you'll be able to see every finely crafted detail."

Wouldn't that be ridiculous? *You've missed the whole point of having a lamp if you've never plugged it in.* But some Christians are living just like that. If we haven't gotten connected to God's power supply, we're basically living like museum pieces sitting on a pedestal, bravely hoping that the outside world will light us up.

Yet God wants so much more ... for all of us.

The Father's plan

We all need to get plugged into God's power supply. His plan is so huge that it's not going to happen any other way!

Here's what I mean. If we were building a few birdhouses, we could get by with sharing a hand drill. But if we're working on a skyscraper, we'll all want access to power tools. As for Father God, he's planning the ultimate construction project of all times. It's going to require ultimate power. That's what Jesus was talking about when he told us:

You will receive power when the Holy Spirit comes upon you.[92]

Do you remember when we talked about the kind of connection that Adam and Eve had with God? They saw him, walked with him, and knew him, face-to-face. and heart-to-heart. Everyday life for them was always empowered. They didn't know how to live any other way. That's the sort of life that God dreams of for you and me. It's the priceless treasure that Adam and Eve lost. It's what Jesus bought back for us. And it's the way we can all start to live when the Holy Spirit lights us up.

We can all become the spiritual equivalent of smartphones, docking with the Holy Spirit to get connected, charged, instructed, empowered. He's our link to the abundant life Jesus was talking about.

Here's how Jesus explained it: "When the Spirit comes, he will guide you into all truth. He will glorify me. He will be with you forever. He lives with you and he will be in you... but you must wait until he comes upon you. I am sending what the Father promised." [93]

The Father's promise

The Father, you see, had promised a package deal, and God takes his promises very seriously. It starts when he tells Isaiah: "The Redeemer will come to Zion," [94] and of course, that's going to be Jesus. But his promise doesn't stop there. Looking into the future that Jesus will secure for us, the Lord goes on to say: "My Spirit, who is on you, will not depart from you." [95] And he tells Joel, "I will pour out my Spirit on all people." [96]

What a massive gift! In the Old Testament, the Holy Spirit only came upon a few people, and they accomplished amazing things. Now, he wants to empower you.

What would happen if you had access to all of his creative energy?

Jesus often collaborated with the Holy Spirit. He was *led* by the Spirit[97], *filled* with the Spirit[98], and *empowered* by the Spirit[99]. He told his followers that getting them connected to the Holy Spirit was a really big deal, and it's vital for us to understand why. "It's for your good that I am going away," Jesus explained. "Unless I go away, the Holy Spirit won't come to you; but if I go, I will send him to you." [100]

Father, Son, and Holy Who?

The Holy Spirit, of course, is the third Person of the Trinity. In Hebrew, he's called *Ruach*; in Greek he is *Pneuma*. Both convey the idea of breath or wind, of a Person who is the very essence of pure life and energy, moving without physical form but with great power, speed, intention, and purpose.[101]

What is he like? He's outrageously loving, irrepressibly joyful, and hysterically funny. He's terrifyingly powerful, but he's also ever so gentle, especially when we're fragile or wounded. He's incredibly wise, and endlessly patient and kind. His life-giving goodness can set every wrong to rights and his powerful peace can still every storm. He's steadfast and faithful. He's utterly purposeful and intentional, and he sees our worst moments as great opportunities to strengthen, comfort, help, and empower us. In fact, the "fruit of the Spirit" that's found in Galatians 5:22-23 is a good start at describing what the Holy Spirit is like.

But no words in any language can fully describe him.
Whatever we think he is, he's so much more!

His personal brand of love, peace and joy are *supercharged*. His tangible presence utterly erases fear. He can make you laugh out loud, right in the middle of impossible difficulties, simply because you know he's right there with you and that he's for you. He's more sensitive than the finest surgical microlaser, precisely cutting away pain that had been lodged deep within us. He can also come in massive, explosive power, as he did when he *personally* raised Jesus from the dead.[102]

The more we know about the Holy Spirit, the more he blows our minds. And we get to experience heart-to-heart connection with him!

When he comes

When Jesus said he would send the Holy Spirit, he was handing us the keys to a life of wonder. Here's *just a taste* of what happens to us when the Holy Spirit comes:

- He walks alongside us.
- He helps us.
- He comforts us.
- He teaches us…in the very moment when we're ready to learn.
- He doesn't judge us. Instead, he lifts us up.
- He points us to Jesus.
- His attention isn't divided. He's *right here* with us.
- He whispers to us about God's plans. Then he makes them happen.
- He shows us how to cooperate with that process.
- He gives us really useful gifts.
- He reproduces *God's actual nature* within us.
- He helps us to become strong, whole, and mature.
- He makes these sorts of resources available to us: enduring love, unshakeable peace, and vibrant, brimming joy.
- He's the One who raised Jesus from the dead. And if we let him, he loves unleashing his massive power into our lives.

The list goes on and on. The Holy Spirit is amazing! [103]

How he comes

So how do we get connected to the Holy Spirit? Does he come upon believers when they first receive Jesus, or is there a "second experience" when he comes in power? Can we pray by ourselves and ask him to come, or should someone else lay hands on us and pray for us? Does he come when we first ask for him? Or do we ask, keep asking, and keep turning to him expectantly as we wait? And what if he has already come? Can we still ask for more?

It's hard to find a single "right" answer to any of those questions, because every one of those experiences can be found in the Bible, and more besides.[104]

I like Randy Clark's perspective. He says: "I believe that the same God who did not make two fingerprints or two snowflakes alike did not intend to make our experience of His Spirit the same for everyone... There appears to be at work here a God who likes diversity, and I suggest that we, too, need to learn to like diversity." [105]

"Be 'being filled' with the Spirit." It's a perpetual, ongoing process; that's the literal translation of Ephesians 5:18. So maybe the key issue isn't how we "got" empowered, but simply that we *get* empowered. Maybe it's time for ALL of us to ask: *"Come, Holy Spirit!"*

Longing for him

The people who are most closely connected to the Holy Spirit don't really get confused by all those complicated theological questions. They don't much care how they first met the Holy Spirit, or when they last did stuff with him. They just want more! They experience what I call *the David Effect.* In the Psalms, David admitted, "At dawn I

search for you. My soul thirsts for you. My body longs for you."
(Psalm 63:1, GW)

Just listen to David's language: Searching. Thirsting. Longing.
Do you hear his desperation?

When we experience true connection to the Spirit of God, our hunger for him can really be that strong. It's like finding the key that opens a lock deep within us. And the only thing we can think is, "I want more, Lord!" Some people say it's like being hardwired to pure love. Others describe a vast sense of peace, or power, or a sense of altered reality and altered purpose, as if they came fully alive in a different sort of way. Usually, his words sound like a still small voice in our hearts. [106] Other times, his presence can be more like a gale-force wind. [107] But always, always, he brings more and better *life*. It's not that we're trying harder. It's just that everything is different, simply because he's here.

Once you've really spent time with the Holy Spirit, you know that you won't ever be the same again. Your whole being starts to vibrate in tune with him. You, too, start experiencing the David Effect.

The Museum of Modern Lighting, Part Two

The light from outside the Museum starts getting dim. Then a massive thunderclap rocks the building.

"Oh, no!" the curator wails, running past us and wringing his hands. "There's a big tour group coming this afternoon. They'll hardly be able to see, and they'll certainly never come back. What a disaster!"

But we'd noticed some strange, flat plates hidden in the floor. It seems the Architect left the Museum with a bit of a surprise. "It's going to be okay," we promise, kneeling down at the curator's feet and pulling back the first plate to reveal... *an electrical outlet.* We plug in the first lamp and watch with delight as its warm glow starts illuminating everything nearby. We do that again and again, turning on one light at a time until the whole room is completely suffused with unspeakable splendor. Their brilliance pours out through the windows and spills across the hillside like a beacon, dispelling the gloom and welcoming everyone. [108]

At first the curator is speechless with indignation, but then he's captivated by the wonder of it all. He turns around and around. At last, he stands perfectly still.

"I see," he whispers.
In that moment, it seems to be all he can say.

Partnering with the Holy Spirit

That's what life is supposed to be like for each of us. The Holy Spirit lights us up, and we become different when we're connected to him.

As we spend time in his presence, he starts changing us. He grows our character, shifts our perspective, gives us gifts, and just plain makes us *more.* He wants to grow us into everything the Father means for us to be.

Don't be startled, though. Just as he comes to us in many different ways, he also expresses himself through us in many different ways as well.[109] Believers who are connected to the Holy Spirit may look very different from each other. And that's okay.

For our part, we ask him to come, we listen, we yield.

What does that look like in our everyday lives? He intends to collaborate with us and empower us. He makes Scripture come alive like never before. Some people say that he gives them flashes of insight, so that they "just know" things they don't have a reason to know. You may hear his voice like a quiet whisper in your heart, or see a quick picture flash on the screen of your mind, or feel a gentle sense of his warmth, reassurance and love. And that's just a start! He speaks to us, blesses us, guides and empowers us in many other ways as well.

When those things happen, it's okay to ask, "Is that you, Lord?" and to check those things out. We're all learning how to listen to the Holy Spirit, and it's going to be a process. Over time, you'll get better at recognizing his voice. It's going to line up with Scripture. And it *always* brings a sense of his presence and a breath of life.

It's a bit like we're dancing together. Some days life seems tough. We ask him to dance us around like little children, with our feet placed trustingly on top of his feet. *But then come the other days.* As we learn more about what the Holy Spirit is like and how he operates, sometimes we get to see truly amazing things, simply because we're hanging out where he is. And in a sense, it doesn't matter which of those two things happens on a particular day. As long as we're partnering with him, good stuff will be going on; stuff we couldn't possibly have done on our own.

That's because as long as we're actively partnering with the Holy Spirit, he's pouring the vast reality of his nature into us and through us. Even on our worst days, we're still being transformed from the inside out by God's kind of love, peace, joy, and patience. *We get to live empowered.*

Who's in charge?

Of course, there's going to be the question of control. Who gets to be in charge, him or you? That issue leaves some people running for cover, because they aren't completely sure that they trust the Lord. He's going to ask us to yield to him and partner with him. I recommend that you vote YES. The Holy Spirit is a genius! His ways and his plans always work out better than ours do.

Jesus was really clear about it. He said, "Keep on asking, and you will receive. Keep on seeking, and you will find… In spite of all your faults, you know how to give good gifts to your children. How much more will your Father in heaven give the Holy Spirit to all who ask!" (Luke 11:9-13, VOICE)

Now, lots of people talk about the Holy Spirit coming "like a dove," because that's how John the Baptist described his coming on Jesus. [110] That's such a lovely image! But it isn't entirely helpful for me. When I think about the Holy Spirit and me, it's obvious that one of us is, in fact, small, nervous, flighty, fickle, and apt to dart away; *but it isn't him.* The Holy Spirit is the One who reached down the roaring maw of Death itself, roared louder still, and pulled Jesus back to life in his resurrected, glorified body. He isn't easily offended. He's massively powerful and dependable, and he's more than able to deal with our puny weaknesses, inabilities and shortcomings. [111]

Often, when we're missing the Lord's presence, it's simply because we've pulled away from him. Maybe something happens that's painful or disappointing. Life, as you know, can get messy. We get hurt, triggered, or offended. Then, instead of turning to the Holy Spirit and asking, "What now?" we turn away. We focus on the offense, rely on our own understanding, and do our own thing for a while.

In the most extreme cases, if someone is determined to live a lifestyle of repeated sin and they actually turn away from the Holy Spirit, they can get into a place that he can't bless. If that's you, you might even think you've gone too far and you're unredeemable. But God doesn't think so! "Where sin increases," according to Romans 5:20 (NIV), "grace increases all the more." Even then, if you're a Christ-follower, the Holy Spirit is still *right there* with you. Whatever sort of mess you're in, he knows the answer. And if you turn to him, ask, and listen, he will help you. And if you're not in a relationship with him yet? Well, that's easy enough to fix.

The place where God dwells

God's plan for us is so much bigger than we've dared to dream.

In the Bible, you can read Solomon's fervent prayer as he dedicates the temple. He's so in awe of God's presence and power. He says, "Even the highest heavens cannot contain you. How much less this temple I have built!" (2 Chronicles 6:18, NIV) Yet Solomon asks the

Lord to come. And what happens next is truly astounding: *Fire falls from heaven. God's actual presence comes and fills the temple, to such an intense degree that the priests can't even get into the door.*[112]

Now, though, we live under an even better covenant.[113]

Now, Paul tells us, "Don't you know? **Your body** is the temple of the Holy Spirit, who comes from God and dwells inside of you." (1 Corinthians 6:19, VOICE, paraphrased)

Look it up. Paul is literally saying: *You have become the Holy of Holies, and you are now the place where God dwells.* And with that, we've come back to God's ultimate construction project.

You see, God is taking a bunch of wildly different, quirky, flawed human beings... *and knitting us together into a living building which can be inhabited by his very presence*[114]. And not only does he intend to dwell in all of us, together. He also intends to dwell in each of us, one at a time.

The Holy Spirit doesn't expect to "visit" with us every once in a while. He means to take up permanent residence, to be with us and empower us from now on. He wants to do life with us. He wants to elevate every one of us, lifting us up into a quality of life that we've hardly dared to dream about. Life changes for us when we truly get that.

The only way to live

Melissa says: "I love being connected to God. I'm living nonstop in a relationship with him, continually. I'm talking to him. He's talking to me. 'Being spiritual' is not a feeling. It isn't based on what I do; it's who I am. Whether I'm driving my kids someplace, or spending time with a friend, or digging in my garden, the Holy Spirit lives in my body. He's with me, and he goes with me wherever I am. I can literally walk into the midst of chaos and still feel his peace."

We too can experience that wonderful reality. It's not what "might be" or what "could be." Instead, it's what *must be*, if we truly want to follow Jesus. Any time you need more *life*, you can turn to the Holy Spirit. You can even stay so close to him that you leave your connection wide open, running flat-out, all the time. He has more than enough juice to do that with all of us, at the same time, continually.

"My life can be busy and complicated," Melissa laughs. "Sometimes it feels like my family of six is going in a hundred different directions. But I've discovered that I carry the Lord's presence with me wherever I go. That's what I want to be—a carrier. I carry his glory! Whether I'm at church, or the grocery store, or the soccer field, the Lord is there with me. That's his promise to every believer. He wants to do life with us."

"Do you actually feel his presence all the time?" I ask her.

"No," she answers honestly. "But I know he's with me all the time, because that's what he promised. Sometimes I feel his presence and I hear his still, small voice deep in my heart, leading me. Sometimes in a situation I just know what he thinks, because I've spent so much time with him. Sometimes I have to pray and wait. Whatever happens, I know I don't have to do things in my own strength anymore. I turn to him. I get to be connected to him."

"It's a different way to live, isn't it?" I observe.
"It's the only way to live," Melissa answers with a grin.

Recap - I Can Live Connected

Every single one of us can get plugged into God's ultimate power source.

Jesus said, "You will receive power when the Holy Spirit comes upon you." That's the essential secret to a successful Christian life. We were never meant to do life on our own! We get to be connected to the Holy Spirit. He's the One who supercharges us, so that we're streaming the life and presence of God in our everyday lives.

He the One who makes us:
Successful.
Fruitful.
Empowered.

Connection: Finding The River

What sorts of things can happen when we partner with the Holy Spirit?
Imagine you're having a dream. At least, you think it's a dream...

You're standing beside the Holy Spirit on a desert cliff as a hot, dry wind blows across your face. You see a couple of ragged-looking little boys playing in the ravine below. There's also a woman hanging laundry nearby; she's even more ragged-looking. Her dress is unkempt, and it doesn't look like she's combed her hair. Glancing at her, you feel revolted, but the Holy Spirit looks at you sharply.

"Don't be so harsh. You have no idea what life is like for her," he says.
You laugh out loud. "Then show me what you know!"
"You couldn't bear it," he warns you. "But I'll give you just a taste."

The images come in a flash. You see a young girl with an open, friendly expression, and she turns into a strong-looking woman. A tall man comes to stand beside her. You recognize their two boys, and you see a little girl as well. You watch sadly as the man disappears and all the light leaves the woman's eyes. You actually *feel the weight* of the broken promises and shattered dreams she carries. Then the little girl vanishes, leaving her mother with empty arms; the hospital was simply too far away. You gasp and fall to your knees as you stare at Holy Spirit, your eyes wide with shock.

"I would help her carry the sorrow," he says quietly. "But she won't let me. She thinks that I don't care. Her faith is all but gone."

Then he looks at you. "Can you believe for her?" he asks. You look at him again, your eyes brimming with tears, and nod. He lifts the cloak off his own shoulders and hands it to you. He points to the rocks on the

163

hillside below, near where the boys are playing.
"Strike the rock," he says; so you take his cloak and strike the rock.
Nothing happens.
"Strike it harder," he instructs you. "Strike it for me."
You think about all her pain as you reach deep within.
WHAM! A tiny crack appears. Nothing else happens.

Then the rocks within your own heart start to break. You suddenly feel the flood of the Holy Spirit's vast, enduring love. Everything he dreams for her. All that he wants to do for her, for her boys. And you turn to him.

"Will you help me?" you ask.
He breaks into a huge grin. "I thought you'd never ask!"

You feel his hands reaching through yours. His presence feels like rushing water, and raging fire, and moving wind, pulsing with energy, all at the same time. You're aware of his anger at this senseless waste and destruction. But you also feel his joy. You feel his strength, his purpose, his determination. It's too much! You have to hide your mind inside of his so that it won't simply melt away.

You look again at that rock.

"NOW!" he says, and together you swing. You strike the rock, but it's not only the rock of the hillside. You're also striking down her pain, her fear, her despair. That's the rock that seals her tomb, leaving her with a dim half-life which is really more of a living death.

The rock before you crumbles, and you feel the earth start to shake.

The Holy Spirit laughs out loud. "If I were you, I'd move," he says with satisfaction as he offers you a hand up. The next moment, a great gush of water bursts forth, and the little boys exclaim with surprise.

"What's going to happen?" you ask.

He really looks very pleased. "The stream turns into a river," he answers. "Good things start to grow. They'll bottle water for their friends. People start asking to stay, and she opens a bed and breakfast. It turns into a small resort. It'll take time, but she'll learn how to be happy again. She'll always have a soft spot for people who are stuck in a dark place. She'll learn how to partner with me to lift them up. Life will never be exactly like it was before, but it will be good again for all of them, very good." He laughs out loud. "So good, in fact, that it lifts up the whole region."

"It's like a dream come true!" you exclaim.
But then your voice trails off as you look deep into his eyes.

"When you meet her, "he says simply, "Tell her that Mary isn't sick anymore. She's very well indeed. She especially loves playing "catch" in the meadow with Jesus and her Grandpa."

The warm glow stays with you as you begin to wake.

Ten years later: You're busy hanging laundry in the washroom. Why did the dryer have to go out? They can't fix it till next week. It's such a pain.

"Hey, come see this!" your son exclaims from the other room. "You said we can take a special vacation next year, right? I was looking for cool places to go. This place sits by a river in the desert. It has such a crazy story. You aren't going to believe it!"

No.

It couldn't be.

Could it?

Jesus stood and shouted... "All you thirsty ones, come to me! Come to me and drink! Believe in me so that rivers of living water will burst out from within you, flowing from your innermost being, just like the Scripture says!" Jesus was prophesying about the Holy Spirit that believers were being prepared to receive.
John 7:37-38 (TPT)

Invitation

*Here's part of Paul's great prayer for the Ephesians.
Let it be his prayer for you.*

I kneel humbly in awe before the Father of our Lord Jesus, the Messiah... and I pray that he would unveil within you the unlimited riches of his glory and favor until supernatural strength floods your innermost being with his divine might and explosive power.

Then, by constantly using your faith, the life of Christ will be released deep inside you, and the resting place of his love will become the very source and root of your life.

... Never doubt God's mighty power to work in you and accomplish all this. He will achieve infinitely more than your greatest request, your most unbelievable dream, and exceed your wildest imagination! He will outdo them all, for his miraculous power constantly energizes you. (Ephesians 3:14-20, TPT)

Hi, Jesus, it's me. You promised that you would send the Holy Spirit to empower me, and I'd like for him to come. I know that he's with me and in me. But I also want his presence to rest upon me. I'm willing to yield control and learn how to do things your way. I say "YES" to your plan.

Come, Holy Spirit!

Living in the YES!

Chapter 9:

My

Life

Matters

ⵊ Laura

Every little kid dreams of making a difference in the world.
You can hear it in their young voices: " I want to be a
doctor." " I want to be a teacher." " I'm going to run for
President!"

For some people, life really works out like that. Maybe
they get a head start with family money, great connections,
or towering talent. Maybe it's been a lot of hard work and a
dash of good fortune.

Others aren't so lucky. The breaks haven't gone their way,
and by now, they've forgotten how to dream. They're either
desperately hoping for just one more tomorrow to wake
up to...or else they're dreading waking up to one more day
like today.

God has a dream, and a destiny, for everyone. But how do
you get there from here? Have you ever been left to
wonder: Do I have to be rich or famous to be significant?

If you've ever asked that question, I have really good
news.
It's time for you to start dreaming again.

You don't have to be rich or famous to be significant!

"About the time our third child was born, we lost everything," Mario remembers. "Marlene and I had both grown up very poor, but after that, we'd built a good life. I owned three businesses. We had our own home and good cars. Then my business failed. Our home, our assets, everything was gone. I had massive debts and no job, no way to pay them off. We had no way to live."

Mario and Marlene watched in horror as the good things in their lives started falling like dominoes. Stunned, they realized they were facing a full-blown catastrophe. They were left to wonder: What do you do when the bottom drops out of your world?

You face a catastrophe head-on, they decided. You look for whatever options are possible, even the ones that would have been unthinkable before. So on Christmas Eve, Mario tearfully said goodbye to his family and his whole way of life, took a huge cut in pay, and left to start work on a ship. "I loved my family so much," he says. "I thought my heart would break. I knew the Lord would have to help me get through this."

171

Then Marlene and their children moved into her aunt's place. (Her aunt wasn't very happy about that, and she wasn't very kind about it, either.) "We had nothing," Marlene admits. "No house, no job, no car, no food. Some nights we went to bed, knowing there wasn't anything in the house to eat the next day."

"How can this be?" That's what Marlene wanted to know. "We'd been serving God for a long time. So I prayed, but it seemed like God didn't even hear me. If he was there, I didn't know it."

Mario and Marlene found themselves facing such a desperate situation. Little did they know that they were perfectly positioned to experience a miracle.

What happened next was truly amazing! I can hardly wait to tell you about the "what." But first, you need to understand the "why." As God's much-loved child, you need to know this, so that you can gain access to a life of miracles for yourself.

We live on a shadowed planet

"How can this be?"
Marlene asked such a great question.
Let's unpack the answer.

In the beginning, God created men and women *in his image*—as powerful beings endowed with great dignity and inherent value. We were given full access to him and empowered to survive in his Presence. We got to truly encounter God, in all of his majesty, glory, and love. We were going to serve together as his co-regents over the Earth. His very nature and his life-giving Presence should have been downloaded into all of us; should have flowed out through us into

172

our world. In time, everything around us would have come to express life, love, power, beauty, wisdom, majesty and justice; because that's what God is like. That was God's plan. It was his dream.[115]

But we said, "No."

The ability to say "no" to God? That's *free will*, and it's God's great gift to us. If you find that idea confusing, just ask any abuse survivor to explain it. They'll help you understand how much you might value having the ability to say "No" to somebody who's a lot more powerful than you are. It's actually a really big deal.

Adam and Eve said, "Thanks, but we're gonna do things our own way. We'll judge for ourselves what's good and what's evil. We're gonna bring our own version of life to the table." (see Genesis 2-3). As they severed their connection to God, his glory and his *life* stopped flowing into them. Those things stopped flowing out through them, as well.

Ever since then, we've been living on a broken, shadowed planet. It's just the reality we live in. We get moments of good, but we also get a lot of disappointment, discord, disease, death, and destruction. Like Mario and Marlene, we can be left feeling completely lost and utterly wretched. What a far cry from the glory God had intended for us, back in the day!

Desperation

Life on a shadowed planet: that's what Marlene and her family were experiencing firsthand. Surviving in a third-world country with no social services and no safety net, they knew the true desperation of hunger. Their children went to sleep every night on the floor in the corner of a tiny little apartment, fully aware of how precarious their situation was.

Marlene, in particular, suffered terribly. "So many times, I felt discouraged and afraid. A lot of times I thought I was going to die, and some moments I really wanted to die. One moment, Satan even whispered in my ear, 'Why don't you just kill yourself?' I had to learn how to battle fear and depression and discouragement, and other things like that."

Can you feel Marlene's desperation? Hear her voice echoing through the night: "Where are you, God? We're hurting. Don't you care?"

There is a place where there are no shadows

All of our human rebellion, and all of our calamity, haven't diminished the glory of God. Throughout history, people have caught the merest glimpses of it.

Now, as a child, I sat through some church services that seemed like they would never end. *Boring!* Off-key songs, a long, tedious sermon, and me, desperately praying for all of it to be over. Is that your idea of church? The Apostle John describes Heaven as a *very* different sort of place. Think about the most thrilling symphony you've ever heard, the most radical rock concert you've ever seen, and the biggest case of being starstruck that you've ever felt. Roll all of them up together, multiply it by about a million, and you might start getting the right idea. For now, sit back for a minute and imagine what it would be like if we had been taken up to Heaven with the Apostle John.[116]

Lord, show us your glory.

We've just entered the doors of God's Great Throne Room. Looking around, we see huge, fearsome creatures and powerful spirit-beings. Massive angels who have spent time in God's Presence radiate power and glory to such a degree that we start trembling uncontrollably as we come near them. Lightning and thunder crackle and shimmer beneath his throne, as the force of his Will waits to go forth and fulfill his Word. What will happen next? The air is thick with expectancy. We're quaking with awe; yet there's such a sense of belonging. We're known and accepted here. God's glory and his love are so tangible that we fall to our knees, wide-eyed with wonder. We join in with the vast throng, laughing with happiness and shouting for joy.

Whatever situations we're facing on Earth, something like that is actually happening in Heaven right now. *Wild celebration, filled with love, hope, joy, and healing!* Misery can't even exist in the Presence of God. In his Presence, there is only glory. Listen to John's eyewitness account:

"I saw One like the Son of Man. His eyes blazed like a fiery flame; his feet gleamed like brightly polished bronze, purified to perfection in a furnace; his voice filled the air and sounded like a roaring waterfall. His face shone a brilliant light, like the blinding sun. ... I saw a throne that stood in heaven and One seated on the throne. Out of the great throne came flashes of lightning, sounds of voices, and peals of thunder.

My heavenly guide brought me to the river of pure living waters, shimmering as brilliantly as crystal. It flowed out from the throne of God. On each bank of the river stood the tree of life, and the leaves ...

provided precious healing for the nations." (Excerpted from Revelation 1:14-16, 4:2-5, 22:1-2, VOICE)

That's just a taste of the glory we were supposed to be linked to.
Life on Earth is such a long way from here.

Liberation

Marlene continues: "The worst part is that our pastor, and our congregation, and our friends who were ministers, all abandoned us! Before that, we'd been very involved. When we had money, we'd been very generous. But now the leaders insisted that we must have committed some secret sin, and they said that God must be punishing us. We became the black sheep, and nobody wanted anything to do with us. I was so hurt. But I knew God wasn't like that. I know that he's good, and I know that he loves me.

"So I was singing and worshiping the Lord at home. As I prayed, his presence would come, and I just wanted to tell him how much I loved him. I had such beautiful encounters with his presence! Then I'd get up every day. I would do the best I could, and I kept asking God to come fill in the rest. I kept asking him to make his goodness real in our lives."

The truth that overshadows the shadow

There's such a gap between the reality of Earth and the reality of Heaven that it's hard to take it in. Things here can be so hard, and they can feel so out of sync. We were never meant to go through this life unaided. We were always supposed to have God's help.

But there is One who felt our suffering. He did something about it; something that you and I, quite frankly, wouldn't have had the strength to do. He left behind the awesome glory of Heaven, so that he could come down here and help us. [117]And help us he did!

"There is a divine mystery—a secret surprise that has been concealed from the world for generations, but now it's being revealed, unfolded and manifested for every holy believer to experience. Living within you is the Christ who floods you with the expectation of glory! Now, because we are united to Christ, we ... have equal and direct access in the realm of the Holy Spirit to come before the Father!" (Colossians 1:26-27, Ephesians 2:18 TPT)

> *Do you remember the heart-link to God that Adam lost?*
> *Jesus bought it back.*
> *Now he gives it freely to everyone who trusts in him.*
> *He truly restored our all-access pass.*

Now, if you're a believer, you've been linked to God again. You're fully forgiven and deeply loved. You have a Redeemer, and he has already paid for your full-price ticket. You have a Father who's looking out for you. And the Holy Spirit? He's right here, ready to guard, guide, and help.

All of that is always true, even while we're living here, on this shadowed planet. It's true when your circumstances are wonderful, and it's still true when they're terrible. It's true whether you feel it or not; it's true whether you see it or not. It's even true when you make the most awful mistakes. This is the powerful truth that overshadows the shadow. This is God's promise to us—and it's his invitation for us to start living a different kind of life.

Resuscitation

Things weren't easy for Mario and Marlene. In fact, for a long time, life was really hard. "One time I felt so discouraged," Marlene says. "I was asking God for a house for my kids and myself, but then I gave up. I started yelling at God, 'Why am I asking you this? You never answer my prayers.' Imagine my shock when I went to church later that day, and a prophet stood up and said, 'You said that I don't answer your prayers. But that prayer you prayed this morning? It has already been answered.'

"I got so excited. 'That's ME!' I thought. 'That's exactly what I said. God heard me. He's talking to ME!' And I went home that night, and found out that it was so. He had answered my prayers. My sister Hiselda called from the US and said, 'Get ready. God gave us the money, and we're building you a house.'

"I had to learn how to not give up," she explains. "How to keep praying until God answered. That's very important. You don't stop praying until the answer comes. I had to keep going when I didn't know if I could."

How do we get back in sync?

Is this confusing enough for you, yet? We live on a shadowed planet; yet we belong to a place where there are no shadows. As long as we're here on the Earth, we're going to keep experiencing those two conflicting realities. The Bible explains it like this: "We're in this world, but we're not of it...we're actually citizens of heaven." (See John 17:11,16; Philippians 3:20.)

My friend Carolyn plays for a major symphony orchestra. (Hi, Carolyn!) She says that once, while they were on tour with a famous piano soloist, the whole orchestra tuned to a pitch that was slightly lower than the piano's tuning. "The way we clashed was awful!" she exclaims. "Brahms must have been turning over in his grave. We thought we'd be producing beautiful harmonies. Instead, we only created chaos and tension."

At that point, in the middle of a concert, they could only grit their teeth and keep on going until they finally reached the end. Sometimes, that's exactly what life feels like for all of us, caught here in this space between two very different realities. It's as if we're hearing two different pieces of music at the same time, and they're very much at odds.

So how do we do it? How do we face the possibility of real trouble, and still live like Overcomers?

There's an important idea we're just beginning to understand, and it's called *synchronicity*. You've experienced it for yourself, if you've ever stood next to an amazing musician and realized that you started singing better, louder, and stronger. Or maybe you shared an exciting idea with a friend, and they truly "got it." In that moment, according to neuroscientists, your two brains started firing in the exact same sequence. They looked like perfect images of each other, electrically. And if you ever spend a lot of time on a horse? Your heart will begin beating in sync with the heartbeat of that great creature. It's not intentional. It's just what happens to all of us, because we're wired for synchronicity.

Living in the YES!

What if you could stop synchronizing your heart and your mind to the discordant, broken world around you, and start synchronizing them to the realities of Heaven, instead?

Determination

Mario and Marlene's son, Eder, picks up their story. "We were living in poverty," he says. "Mom and Dad were basically working to pay off their debts, not to eat and survive. We started learning how to expect miracles, though. When we didn't have any food, Mom would get all of us together. We'd bow before God and start praying for food. The first time she did that, she had already stayed up praying all night! Eventually, a friend would come and bring us enough food for a week. We started seeing God do one miracle after another, just like that."

Experiencing congruence... and confluence

As believers, we get to experience synchronicity with God. Jesus gave us the key to the mystery when he said, "The kingdom of God is within you." (Luke 17:21) That's how the restoration begins. Your human spirit gets reconnected to God's Spirit, and *life* starts flowing, deep within you. Then it starts bubbling up from your spirit and seeping into your mind. You start seeing things in new ways. Your feelings start shifting. Your values change, and then you start making different choices. You start letting go of the old garbage that was blocking you from experiencing the rich inner *life* that God intends for you.

As that process keeps happening, you become more whole. You're being renewed or, quite literally, *transfigured* (according to Romans

180

12:2). Your life comes more and more into alignment with who you were always meant to be. *You start experiencing congruence.*

But that's not all! Even while we're still imperfect, even while we're still living on this broken, shadowed planet, things within us can actually start working according to God's original design. Each of us can become an easy conduit for the life, the love, and the Presence of God to flow through.

It's like God is going somewhere, and you find that you're going to the same somewhere. If your life is a little stream, it joins up and starts flowing together with God's mighty river. *His grace is flowing where you're going. And when that happens... well, you've just found confluence.* That's when it's on, baby. Miracles start breaking out all over the place. You start actually living the life God dreams of for you!

Regeneration

Now you can understand what happened with Mario and Marlene. It's not that their circumstances changed. Instead, in the midst of terrible difficulties, they found a way to sync their lives with God's Presence. As they did, he comforted them, helped them, and filled them with a sense of purpose and joy. That's when life around them started changing.

Finding out who you really are

What makes your life matter? Maybe you think it's all about what you have, what you can do, or who you know. And all of those things are important! That's how lives, communities, and even civilizations are built. But that sort of life has limitations. You can "have it all" and still

181

feel empty. Or, as Mario and Marlene discovered, you can lose it all and be left with nothing. There's another truth which you really need to know, and it goes like this:

What you do, matters; but how you do it matters more. Just think about Mario. How desperate he must have felt! Yet he kept turning to the Lord for strength and help. He kept living with honor, consistency, and integrity, even when it seemed like everything in his life had gone sideways. And even though he didn't know it at the time, it turns out that he'd become a living, breathing "love letter" from God: love and faith wearing human skin, written and sent to any number of people who never would have opened (or trusted) a Bible. [118]

> *And now we come to the most important truth of all.*
> *What you do, matters, and how you do it matters more.*
> *But who you are matters most of all.*

You are, in reality, a Son or Daughter of the Most High God. [119] You've been made, and you're being remade, in his image. You're linked to him. You get to share his heart, his values, his thoughts. You get to share your dreams with him. And just ask; he'll share his dreams with you, too. That's the sort of stuff that was actually going on with Marlene. She thought she was simply praying about food for her family. In reality, she was learning how to connect, yield, and partner with God. *Just think about it. God's resources, his contacts, his abilities. And he's your Daddy!* God was growing Marlene from the inside out, making her more *real*, and getting her truly connected to himself.

Think about how a person's life changes when that happens. Think about how it changes the world.

Restoration

Mario says: "One day while I was on the ship, another man came to me. 'I'm headed home,' he said. 'When I get there, I want to find a church. I want to live before God the way you do.' I was so surprised. Before that, he'd never said anything. But God says that he makes us 'living letters.' He speaks through us, even when we don't know what he's doing.

"Then, after I had been at sea for thirteen years, the CEO of a large company called me. He said, 'Get off of those ships and come home. I'm giving you a job here.' Nine months later, I started my own company. Slowly, God started returning all those material things that we had lost."

Learning a new way to run the race

"Run the race that has been set before you," the Bible advises us in Hebrews 12:1. So here we are. We're down on the track, warming up. All around us, people are stretching, flexing, shaking off the tension, jumping lightly on the balls of their feet. Then the Holy Spirit strolls up. "I'm here to help you today," he says with a grin. "Oh!" you reply. "That's... uh... great?" You're not quite sure about this.

Humming pleasantly to himself, the Holy Spirit takes out some things that look suspiciously like the shimmering, heavenly version of bungee cords. Imagine your consternation as he starts lashing his right leg to your left leg, from your ankles to your knees. "We're going to do a three-legged race today," he remarks casually. "We'll be running in sync. It'll be great!"

"What?" you splutter. "Running together like that is really hard! That's not going to help me. It's going to slow me down. Everyone else will be going as fast as they can. We're sure to come in last!" But you're wasting your breath. You're not sure if he even hears you; he seems so unmoved and undeterred.

The starting pistol cracks, and everyone else takes off like a rocket. You barely make it off the starting blocks. At first, you're limping, tripping, going face-down, and generally making a spectacle of yourself, tightly tied to somebody that no one else can even see. But then you start getting the hang of it: learning when to go, when to pause, and how to move in tandem with God. That's when you really start to fly. This is effortless for him, and the two of you start surging forward. "Wow! I didn't know I could go so fast," you think. "This is fun!"

Jubilation

"Now," Marlene says with relish, "We will tell you about the season of miracles." This story was twenty-one years in the making. Time and again, other people brought them food when they had nothing and they prayed. The rest of their massive debt was canceled. God moved on different people to build a house and give it to them; to furnish it; and to provide, not one, but two new cars, when they could not have afforded any of those things. Their four sons all have a deep faith in God. They're all University graduates. Two are engineers who work with their Dad, and two are successful classical musicians.

They've seen God do one miracle after another when they prayed: physical healing, healing of mental disorders, provision. One of the first big miracles was a family member getting healed. After that, their entire extended family started becoming Christians. Now they pastor a church where other hurting people can come to be helped, loved, and connected with the Lord. They also coordinate a food bank and a clothing ministry.

A family who once lived in a little corner found out that if they had nothing but Jesus, they had everything. The world is a different place, simply because they're here. It's like they've become lightning rods, places where God's presence can dwell and his glory can fall.

Mario and Marlene didn't merely experience breakthrough for themselves. Instead, they've become breakthrough, for so many other hurting people. But it hasn't changed them. For them, it's always, only, now and forever, all about Jesus. His love for them; their love for him; his love for others.

"I know what it's like to sleep on a floor," her son Eder says with easy grace. "And I know what it's like to be flown somewhere first class to give a musical performance. It's all the same to me! The best part of life truly is experiencing God's love. Everything else? It's just stuff."

Aren't you glad Mario and Marlene didn't give up on life when things were hard? After all, you never have any idea what God is about to do... or what he wants to do through you.

Awakening to our destiny

As long as we're here on this Earth, we may, indeed, be caught between two conflicting realities. Yet at the same time, we share one amazing destiny.

"We are like common clay jars that carry this glorious treasure within, so that the extraordinary overflow of power will be seen as God's, not ours. Though we experience every kind of pressure, we're not crushed. At times we don't know what to do, but quitting is not an option... God has not forsaken us. We may be knocked down, but not out.

"Every detail of our lives is continually woven together to fit into God's perfect plan of bringing good into our lives, for we are his lovers who have been called to fulfill his designed purpose. For he knew all about us before we were born and he destined us from the beginning to share the likeness of his Son. This means the Son is the oldest among a vast family of brothers and sisters who will become just like him."

(2 Corinthians 4:7-10, Romans 8:28-29, TPT)

Now we're finally starting to catch a glimpse of our ultimate destiny:
We get to become like Jesus.

It's time for God's people to wake up. His idea of destiny is a whole lot bigger than ours has ever been.

Becoming mature sons and daughters

You see, God can and does change things around you. But his greatest will isn't expressed when he merely changes your circumstances. It's expressed as you collaborate with him, and let him change you.

God wants to strengthen your faith and help you to have lots of it. He wants to grow your spirit and teach you how to walk with him. You'll become stronger and more whole. Your spiritual "armor" [120] will get upgraded. Then, the next time you face a crisis, it won't have quite the same power to overwhelm you. And the next time, and the next, and the next... You'll start learning how to walk hand-in-hand with our miracle-working God. And how about that? That's exactly what we were supposed to be doing to begin with.

Right here, right now, in the middle of two conflicting realities, God is actively moving in your life. He wants to help you become his mature son or daughter, a re-created being who carries his spiritual DNA, bears his image and shares his heart. Then he wants to partner with you and help you to do life, here on this shadowed planet, while you are sheltered under his shadow. [121]

Revelation

"I used to ask God to rescue me from my circumstances," Marlene admits. "At first, I didn't understand why he didn't do that. But now I see that he did so much more! God has plans and purposes that he doesn't need to tell you. You just need to learn how to walk with him. Now, when I find people who are facing terrible difficulties like I did, I don't tell the Lord, 'Please take this test away from them.' Instead, I pray, 'My Lord, strengthen this person, so that he can be an overcomer.'" *

What about you?

What will your life be like when all of this becomes true in you? You're partnering with God and doing life together with him. You're

---

* You'll find more of this family's amazing story on page 293.

living lovingly, joyfully, and hopefully. His presence is invading the little corner of the world where you live, simply because you live there, and he lives in you. It'll be like you have one foot firmly planted on the Earth, and the other planted firmly in Heaven. You'll get to become a bridge, so that things which are happening *there* start taking shape *here*, as well.

Imagine FAITH walking into the room when you do, so that people sit up a little straighter and think, "Is that true? God really cares about me, too?" Imagine HOPE walking into the room when you do, and depression walking out... not because you said anything, but simply because you're there. I've known a few people who carry God's presence like that. Imagine LOVE walking into the room when you do, so that nobody you meet ever has to feel invisible or unimportant. Obviously, you can't possibly do any of that on your own. You'll have to be linked to God every step of the way. That's when you'll find you're living the best kind of life.

Do you remember Jo Moody from Chapter Two? On that wonderful night when she got healed, her friend kept whispering, "Do you think that man who prayed for you was an angel?" Now Jo prays for a lot of people, and I'd bet some of them ask that same question about her. Maybe someday, they'll ask it about you.

Whatever happens next, though, from this point on you're always going to know the truth:

I'm the one that Jesus loves, and I'm doing this life together with him. He says that my life matters!

Consider this God's personal invitation.
Come partner with him and start living in his dream come true.

Recap: My life matters

You don't have to be rich or famous to be significant.

As believers, we constantly find ourselves living in two conflicting realities. On the one hand, we live on a broken, shadowed planet. At the same time, we ourselves are overshadowed by the reality of God's presence, love, and acceptance.

Even while we're facing that first hard reality, God invites us to be linked and synced to him. In fact, you can actually become a bridge, calling down God's presence and provision, his "true riches," into the hurting world around you.

And you are significant, simply because God says you are. Even though you may face terrible pressures in this world, they can't prevent you from entering God's presence and literally becoming his agent on the Earth.

When you do... you don't merely experience God's Kingdom. Instead, you become the Kingdom.

Connection: The Secret Garden

The Bible says we can draw life from God's presence. That changes us—
and it changes the world. What would it look like if we could see that?

Tonight, you just felt drawn to Heaven. You don't have any special plans. You're just walking in the cool of the garden, enjoying the stillness. It's so restful here, so saturated with the presence of God. The cares of everyday life fall away, and you soak in his gentle love.

Then you realize you've ended up in a different part of the garden, and a new scent floats in on the air. It's intoxicating, pungent and sweet, and it evokes such longing within you. *What is it? Where is it coming from?* You turn this way and that, searching for the source. Then you round a corner, and your face lights up as you see that the Holy Spirit is already there. "I've been waiting for you," he says with a smile. "Come."

He leads you to a door beneath an arched trellis, unlocking it with the touch of his hand. "This is MY garden," he tells you.

You stand stock-still and gasp in awe as you gaze up at the magnificent tree that's rising before you. It's tall and strong and lovely. There's no breeze tonight, yet its leaves rustle gently, tossing lightly this way and that as if it's actually alive. But what truly captures your attention is the fruit. It's unlike anything you've ever seen before: every orb gleaming softly in the night, as if it's lit from within. That has to be where the wonderful fragrance is coming from. You turn to the Holy Spirit, asking without words: *What is the secret of this place?*

He nods in the direction of the tree. "Its roots grow near the River of Life," he observes. "When trees grow there, this always happens. The life from the River works its way into the fruits. They would be sweet on their own, but only the River can make them grow like this."

Then he looks straight at you and your breath catches. You don't know what's about to happen, but you know that something is about to change. A Moment is taking place.

"This tree is your life," he says simply.

"The things you're doing on Earth have eternal significance. They matter there, and they matter here, because you're drawing life from the River. Always remember that. When you're back on Earth, it won't matter what stinking pit or cesspool you find yourself in. As long as you keep your roots in the River, you will always produce living fruit."

You're quiet for quite a while, trying to take it all in.
"Thank you for showing me," you finally whisper.

Then you impulsively add: "Can we wait just a little longer before we have to go back?" And he answers: "Of course!" With a grin, he taps you on the shoulder and then he's gone. "I'm on the move," he calls back. "Catch me if you can!" You laugh helplessly and run after him.

"Blessed is the one who trusts in the Lord... They will be like a tree planted by the water that sends out its roots by the stream. It does not fear when heat comes; its leaves are always green. It has no worries in a year of drought and never fails to bear fruit."
Jeremiah 17:7-8 (NIV)

Chapter 10:

When

We Live

In The YES!

*Laura*

We've been on quite a journey, haven't we? For me, it's
been an intense three-year process, starting about six
months before God healed me of the brain injury." I want
you to write a book," the Holy Spirit said, and I started
laughing." Good one, God! I mean, you're obviously kidding,
right? I can barely write a grocery list. How on earth am
I going to manage a book?"

Turns out, he wanted to write this book "into" me before
he wrote it through me, and I have been changed. At first,
I kept acting like the end product was going to be a thing
(the book.) God, on the other hand, kept acting like the end
product was going to be a person (me.) Once I caught on,
things in my life made more sense, and I did better at
cooperating with him.

I'm giving you a heads-up about that, because it's
probably going to be true for you as well. God isn't trying
to make you smarter, as if you needed to "perform" in
order to earn his affection or approval. Instead, he's going

to be writing truth and love into your heart, and growing YOU as a person. You are his much-danced-over son or daughter, and you have a Father who loves you very much. This is really just a launching point.

So... welcome to the process.
And... prepare to be loved on by God!

Living in the YES!

What's going to happen when all of this truth becomes alive in you?

Well, we've gotten to the end, and now you know what I know about living in God's YES. Just make sure you remember: These aren't merely theoretical truths or nice ideals. Instead, they're entirely real, the rock-solid foundation on which you can build a great life. One that thrives like crazy in the good times. One that still endures, even on your worst days.

- **God is truly good**. He's amazing; and really knowing him changes everything else.
- **He isn't mad at you**. He's still good, even when life feels bad.
- **You don't have to earn his love**. Instead, he gives it to you freely. You don't ever have to do enough good to be "good enough" for him.
- **He welcomes you into his family**. You're not just his faithful servant. You're his beloved child!
- **You are really forgiven**. You're not defined by your mistakes or

197

shortcomings anymore. Instead, you are clean and forgiven, and standing under the waterfall of God's grace.

- **He has given you his righteousness**. Jesus bought the right to put you to rights.[122] He has given you a new nature—his nature. Now he's making you real, true, well and whole, so that you can fully enjoy living as your true self.

- **You can live connected to him**. The Holy Spirit will lead you and guide you. He's the one who empowers you and sets you up for abundant living.

- **Your life matters**. You don't have to be rich or famous to be significant. The world is a better place because you're here!

Every one of these truths is the birthright of every believer. If you're trusting in Jesus as your Savior, every one of them is available to you. You don't have to earn them. Instead, you get to step up and claim them as your prize. Jesus paid an unimaginable price, so that he could have the right to give you these priceless gifts as an inheritance. He did it because of the way that he loves you.

Experiencing God's faithfulness. His goodness. His love! Knowing him and being deeply connected to him. These astounding truths are a game-changer for all of us.

Life changes when you know God that way...
And we can all know God that way.
I know what that's like, because it happened to me.

Is this for real?

It was about three years after the brain injury when my switch got flipped. I'd been working up quite a temper one day, telling the Lord how hard my life was, when a picture flashed quickly across the screen of my mind. It was like I could see a happy little waterfall, situated in the same room where I was, just a little bit behind me. It came down out of the ceiling, cheerfully splashing and puddling, and then it disappeared into the floor.

Now, don't worry. I wasn't going crazy, and—thank goodness—we didn't have an actual plumbing leak! But I could see this picture in my mind so clearly that it felt very real. I was so startled that I broke off in midsentence and stopped complaining.

That same picture persisted in my mind for about two months. It was almost like the little waterfall had started following me around. It became more and more vivid to my mind's eye, until I could almost smell the ozone in the air. "What are you saying, Lord?" I kept asking. Then I found this Scripture:

"For no matter how many promises God has made, they are "Yes" in Christ." (2 Corinthians 1:20, NIV)

I came to believe that I was looking at a visual representation of God's "YES." And in a spiritual sense, I found out that it was, in fact, very real. A tangible link to God's presence was quite literally following me around, and I could access it at any time. First I had to make a choice, and stop obsessing over whatever was freaking me out. Then I'd turn my attention away from my fear, and tune in to God's presence instead. When I did, I could *actually experience* his

199

peace. He soothed me. He strengthened and empowered me, so I could go back to dealing with my very tough reality. That even worked in the worst moments, when it felt like my brain was screaming in agony. It's like God was literally holding me, for however long it took until the pain subsided.

Now, maybe that sounds strange to you. I can only tell you that it really happened. Sometimes when I prayed for other people, they felt it, too. That's why I was praying so fervently for a complete stranger, six months later, on the night when Jesus came and healed me.

The greater gift

Because of the brain injury, I'd been living for years with such painful limitations. *Couldn't do this. Can't do that.* At first, it felt like the wellspring of my life and happiness had been shut off forever. But then I found out it simply wasn't so! I'd just been drinking from the wrong well.[123] You see, the best kind of life never did flow from me. Not from my will. Not from my intelligence or my creativity. Not from where I went, what I had, or what I did. Nothing like that!

> *True life…*
> *It always, only, ever, comes from God.*
> *That's his priceless gift…*
> *And he offers it freely to all of us.*

All of these great truths were still completely real, completely true, and completely available to me, even while I was in a very tough place. And they turned out to be far more than mere words on a page. Instead, they became like a fire, burning in my heart. They were the lifeline linking me to the very tangible presence of God.

200

Discovering that? It changed everything.

Now, you may be smarter than I am. Maybe you already knew ALL of the things we've talked about. Or maybe you only needed a chapter or two, or just a single paragraph, in order to grow. But me? I was hard core! I desperately needed to learn *every single one* of these great truths, not just with my head, but with my flesh and blood and bone. I'm so glad God invested in spending time with me, so that all of this could start becoming real in my life. Being healed was amazing, and I thank him every day for that incredible gift. But I'm even more glad that before he healed my brain, he healed the broken places in my heart.

Learning how to live in his YES... that truly was the greater gift.

Now I want you to meet my friends Peter and Anne. Like me, they too had an encounter with God's YES. They'd always seen themselves as normal, everyday Christians. Then God started redefining "normal Christianity" for them.

Peter and Anne

Peter explains it like this. "I'd have to say that we started out, really, as unbelieving believers. We'd always said that the Bible was true, but we never would have expected the things that happened in the Bible to happen in our lives. Then we went to this conference, and we found out that there's more to life with God than we'd ever dreamed of."

Anne laughs and adds: "You can't imagine two people who were more like fish out of water than we were! We came from a traditional church where people were very reserved. People in this place were laughing and crying. They were responding to something we couldn't see or feel. Laypeople[124] were praying for each other, and they were getting healed! To be honest, we'd always sort of had our doubts about people who carried on like that.

"But we were surprised by what we found out. These people saw their faith walk as more than an intellectual exercise. It was also relational, and it was a real part of their everyday lives. The speakers gave us some great teaching about the Biblical basis for healing, and for why they did the things that they did. What they said was smart, and it was scriptural. It gradually dawned on me that we'd been wrong. These people were more than just "emotional Christians." They not only knew the Bible; they were living like it was actually true! So many of them were having experiences that we weren't having. At first, Peter was a little bit put out, but I realized I was hungry. I felt like it was Passover, and we were being passed over. I wanted what they had."

On the last day of the conference, Peter had a first-person encounter with the Holy Spirit. He says, "It felt like I had pure liquid love flowing all through me, and the only thing I could say was, 'Thank you, Jesus.' Anne didn't have such a dramatic experience, but by the time the conference was over, we both felt like we were ten feet off the ground, full of the Holy Spirit."

Peter continues, "I felt like I'd been born again, again. I'd been a believer for thirty years, yet I was experiencing things I'd never seen or even knew existed. It almost seemed like, before this, I'd been deceived. Before, I hadn't understood that 'having faith' was anything more than having the right mindset. Now it was like a veil had been lifted, and I was seeing these things for the first time. All this stuff was Biblical. It was available, even though we hadn't known about it. It changed me."

Anne adds, "I'd always loved hearing the stories about Jesus and all the things he did. But then as you grow up, you try to explain why those things don't still happen today. Now that we'd gotten a more complete Biblical understanding of the Holy Spirit and our power as believers, I felt like I was a kid again, saying, 'It WAS true! I knew it all along!'" *

What the YES looks like for them

Peter and Anne went home and started connecting with God in an entirely new way. They already knew the Bible, but now it started coming to life, first in them and then through them. They've learned how to stand on God's promises, in faith, until they become reality. They've seen miracles happen when they prayed. They've seen other people encounter Jesus, and their own lives have been transformed. Now they love to share this kind of experience with others. They're convinced that THIS is what's meant to be "normal Christianity." They think God wants to make this kind of life available to every believer.

---

* To hear more from Peter and Anne, turn to page 300.

Peter says, "We've never looked back. I tell people: You can forget your house, your 401k, your IRA, your job. Nothing matters like this does. Whenever that liquid love is flowing through you, that's all you need. You can live on it. You can run on it." Anne adds, "It's just hard to take it in, how generous God is. Be hungry for him, because there's so much more to this life than you know. That's what we started calling this experience: 'the more.' It's here for you, too. Ask him for more."

Here's how the Bible explains it: "Now all of us, with our faces unveiled, reflect the glory of the Lord as if we are mirrors; and so we are being transformed, *metamorphosed*, into His same image from one radiance of glory to another, just as the Spirit of the Lord accomplishes it." (2 Corinthians 3:18, VOICE)

Finding the wider world

For all of us, life can be busy and messy. It can be glorious or disappointing, even painful at times. We can have days when we're so proud of ourselves... and days when we're so not. But through it all, our steady constant is the reality of God's vast, enduring love.

When we learn how to live out of that truth, our circumstances no longer have the power to define us. Even in the worst of difficulties, we can turn to God and experience his help, his comfort, and his guidance. We can pray with confidence, because we know his heart. We can lean on him for strength until the answer comes.[125] We become transformed. Then the world around us becomes transformed, as our lives become echoes and reflections of his glorious nature.

Life changes when we learn how to get connected to God's presence like that, and how to stay connected. We begin living in that wider world beyond our selves, the world we talked about at the start of the book. It's the place where ordinary becomes extraordinary. Amazing things become possible for us, simply because we're connected to the Presence of God...and *nothing* is impossible for him.

We can all live like that!
Connected to God.
Living in response to him...
Living in his YES.

Life is still going to be imperfect, and so are we. Some days may feel like good days, and other days may be really tough. Yet despite all of that, every single one of our days can be filled with *life* when we discover who we really are. We don't have to just "make do" anymore We never have to barely scrape by, merely saying, "I'm doing well... under the circumstances."

You remember that, now. You don't have to live "under your circumstances," because you're under the Blood of Jesus. You're going to be an overcomer, because The Overcomer lives inside of you!

You're so significant to the Lord. He has set your place at his table, and he has saved your place in his heart. As far as he's concerned, nobody else can ever fill either one. In one way, he shares his love with all of us. But in another way, there's a love that he has reserved for you alone.

What will the YES look like for you?

What do you think? Can we go on one more imaginary journey?

The day starts out like an ordinary day. But then it happens...that thing you've been dreading. "NO!" you wail. "Please not yet. Please not now." But life, as we know all too well, doesn't await our convenience; and now, suddenly, here you are.

At first, you're tempted to react in the same old ways; but then you remember that you're living in God's YES. You think about Jo Moody, and you say, "Hey, wait a minute! God really is good, and he really does love me." You think about Alex praying for Miss Julia, and you remember God's amazing compassion. "He knows what this feels like, and he cares about me," you whisper. You spend some time in God's presence, like Marlene did, and you start feeling a little better. Then you can almost hear Ian asking, "I don't know why this happened, Lord, but I need you. Will you comfort me? Will you help me? Show me what I need to do next." So that's what you do, too.

About that time, a couple of "friends" show up. They think God must be punishing you for something. "What have you done?" they demand. At first, you feel hurt. Then you remember what Rachel and Vijay learned. "I'm really forgiven!" you exclaim. "And I don't ever have to do enough good to be good enough for God. Jesus already did that for me. Because of what he did, I have a secure place in God's heart."

Then you go on. "Whatever mistakes I've made, God is going to help me deal with them," you affirm. "He'll help me to see what they are, so I can own up to them and say that I'm sorry. He'll help me do my

206

best to put things to rights. He'll help me deal with the earthly consequences, and he'll help me to grow, so I can do better next time. As for the things that weren't my mistakes—the things someone else did, and the things that just happened? He's going to help me deal with those, too. It may take a minute, but no situation has ever been too big for God to handle."

Up to this point, you've been sort of hunched over. But now you think about Ellen and Melissa, and you start standing a little straighter. "You see, I'm not just God's servant!" you roar. "I'm his beloved child! I can't possibly face this situation alone, because I can't even BE alone. The Lord is always right here with me. No matter what happens to me, no matter why it happens, he's going to walk through it with me, every step of the way. He's going to help me."

Finally, Tula's story leaps into your mind, and you stand stock-still, as your face reflects the dawning wonder of it all.

"In fact," you go on, "God believes in me so much that he has actually given me his DNA. He's gonna help me learn whatever I need to, grow however I need to, and become whoever I need to. The same power that raised Jesus from the dead lives in me! As long as there's breath in my body, I have hope, because God is here. And when this life is over, well, it only gets better. As far as God is concerned, I can actually come out of this thing more whole than I was when I went into it."

Then you get really excited. "Hey! Maybe God is going to show up and set somebody else free, too. I wonder what that's gonna look like?"

One of your friends gets offended, and they leave in a huff. The other one timidly asks, "Do you think God could ever care about me like that?" That's when you grin broadly and say, "Let's sit down for a minute. We need to talk."

We're going on a journey

We started this grand adventure by looking at a powerful scripture:

"Make the crooked road wide and straight for our God. Where there are steep valleys, treacherous descents, raise the highway; lift it up; bring down the dizzying heights. Fill in the potholes and gullies, the rough places. Iron out the shoulders flat and wide.

The Lord will be, really be, among us. The radiant glory of the Lord will be revealed. All flesh together will take it in. Believe it. None other than God, the Eternal, has spoken." (Isaiah 40:3-5, VOICE)

As we've traveled together through these pages, I hope this Scripture has come alive for you. I hope we've filled in at least a few of the potholes and gullies in your life. I hope some of the boulders have been removed, and the rockfall swept away, so that the path between you and God is clear and straight and wide. He loves you so much! He not only wants to come for you; he wants to BE with you. He truly does want to "do life" together with you from now on.

That's when God's glory really will be revealed. First, he'll reveal it to you, so that you're awestruck by the magnitude and wonder of it all. Then, as time you've spent with him transforms you, he'll start revealing his glory through you. Just like Mario, you'll become God's "living love letter" to the world, written not in ink but in the human spirit.

As we've said before, that truly is the adventure of a lifetime.

God's grand invitation

Maybe you know the Lord well, or maybe you don't really know him yet. Maybe you've kept him at arm's length, settling for a "good" life lived by moral principles. But no matter! In any of those cases, God himself is inviting you to come closer and experience something more.

We catch just a glimpse of the burning, fiery glory of who God is. We begin to comprehend the massive price he paid to redeem us, and the breathtaking invitation he's offering. He's inviting you to know him as he is, and to really, truly be connected to him.

How are you going to respond?

Some people imagine falling asleep and meeting God in a dream, or going into a trance-like state and having an open vision. Those things can and do happen, but that's not how Zechariah described his encounter with the Lord. He said, "The Messenger-Angel ... called me to attention. It was like being wakened out of deep sleep." (Zechariah 4:1, MSG)

That's exactly what God wants to do for each of us. He awakens us from the sleepy stupor with which we go through life. *Right here, right now,* he awakens our spirits to the vast reality of his love, his Presence, and his amazing grace. And then...there we are, blinking in astonishment at the wonders we suddenly start perceiving all around us.

"Wake up, dear one."

He's whispering to you right now.
Can you hear his voice?
Can you feel the wind of his mighty Presence blowing across your heart?

God himself is inviting you in.

You're his masterwork, and he has great plans for your life...
but you can only accomplish them together with him.
Come to the river that flows from his great Presence,
and drink.

Come deeper.
Deeper.
Deeper still!

What adventures does he have in store for you?
Won't it be wonderful to find out!

Recap: When we live in the YES

What will it look like when all of this truth comes to life in you? God is inviting YOU to come even closer to him, and to live from now on in his YES. This vast, wonderful reality shapes and redefines our lives. We begin to discover that absolutely nothing can separate us from God and his amazing, transforming love. Our hearts begin to burn within us, until we echo the Apostle Paul's great cry:

"Oh! That I might know him!" *

- God is truly good.
- He isn't mad at me.
- I don't have to earn his love.
- He welcomes me into his family.
- I am really forgiven.
- He has given me his righteousness.
- I can live connected to him.
- My life matters!

Really, these are all just different aspects of one overarching truth. If you only remember one thing, remember this.

God is faithful, loving, and good. And he loves me!

Connection: Walking The Streets Of Heaven

Imagine the Lord has asked you to come in for a moment.
He wants to have a word with you.

As you walk down the street in Heaven, heads turn in your direction. Faces light up as angels, walking past, greet you respectfully.

"What's going on?" you wonder. Your hearing is super sharp here, which is very cool, so you tune into what they are saying. You hear: *"Greatly loved"* — *"Overcomer"* — *"Faithful"* — *"Victorious"* — *"Looks so much like the Father walking down the street, you can just see the family resemblance!"* You smile secretly and walk a little straighter. Your pace quickens as you draw close to the meeting place. And your face truly lights up as you enter the door and find yourself enfolded in Jesus' arms.

"I'm so glad to see you!" he exclaims. "Let me just love on you for a minute. Then we're going to meet up with the Holy Spirit and put our heads together. I can't wait to tell you what we're about to do!"

For he knew all about us before we were born and he destined us from the beginning to share the likeness of his Son. This means the Son is the oldest among a vast family of brothers and sisters who will become just like him. Romans 8:29 (TPT)

Blessings!

As you continue on your life's journey, know that a vast crowd of supporters is cheering you on. You've already gotten a hint of Father God's great heart for you. On top of that, Jesus himself is personally interceding for you in Heaven right now. The Holy Spirit is praying over you, as well. Past generations have already prayed for you, for God's will to become reality in your life.[126] Then there's the Apostle Paul; you can find his prayer for you in Ephesians 1:15-20 & 3:14-20.

Every person who shared their story in this book has been praying for you. So have the pre-readers and focus group members. I think Stefanie (see page 256) pretty much spoke for all of them when she prayed:

Lord, everyone who hears this story has a story of their own. You are also the author of their story, and you're writing a beautiful chapter in their life. Lord, let them know that you provide constant companionship and comfort, and with you, there's always hope. It just flows from who you are. Let that become a reality for them. In Jesus' name, Amen.

Now I want to add my small part to that great symphony of prayer:

Lord, thank you for every single person who has walked through these pages. Their name is written on your heart! Awaken their spirit, more and more, to that grand reality. Bring your good will to pass in their life. Cause your joy, your love, your peace and wholeness to rule within them. Make them part of your great Kingdom—not just in eternity, but here and now. May they be a beautiful part of what you're doing today! Whatever joys or challenges they're facing, assure them that you are right there with them, and you're absolutely reliable. You have begun a great work within them, Lord, and you'll keep working on it for as long

213

Living in the YES!

as they draw breath.[127] Until the glorious day when they meet you face to face, let them know that they truly can live in your YES!

Want to join the movement? Ask the Lord who you can be praying for!

AFTERWORD:

How

Heaven

Is Like Hawaii

Living in the YES!

It's true! To my mind, Heaven is a lot like Hawaii. But I'm not talking about lush greenery, gentle breezes or delicious fruits (although I have to admit: that does sound pretty heavenly). For me, the reason is very personal.

Let me explain.

The summer after our daughter Ellen finished high school, we took a family trip to Hawaii. We'd been saving and planning for many years. We bought the tickets and booked the condo. We looked up places we thought we'd like to go. We had a budget for eating in, and a budget for eating out. A room was set aside just for her.

But in the end, she decided that she didn't want to go.

We begged. We pleaded. We cajoled. We described how wonderful it would be. Right at that moment, things were fairly stressful between us, but we told her that we wouldn't have to "work anything out" or talk about anything difficult. We just thought that it was going to be a wonderful time, and we wanted her to be where we were.

But Ellen was still dealing with so many issues from her past in Russia, and I don't think she had quite decided what sort of place we were going to have in her life. Eventually, we realized that the only way we could express our love for her was by respecting her choice not to be with us.

We went on the trip and had a fabulous time with the rest of our kids. Hawaii must be one of the most beautiful places on Earth! But we all had an ache in our hearts for the person we were missing, and we knew that there should have been another place at the table. I especially remember the comfort we found as we walked into The Painted Church. (It's an old mission on the Big Island.) It felt like we had just walked into the place where Love dwells, and we instantly knew that we were encountering the tangible presence of God. We stayed there for a long time as he comforted our hearts. We asked him to love on Ellen and keep her safe.

And that's how Heaven is like Hawaii.

It's such a wonderful place! We're all *ohana* there; we're all family. God's love is so tangible that it permeates the very air itself, and his unveiled presence literally lights up all of Heaven. We can actually walk with him, hand in hand. We can be together forever with people we love.

You can't get there on our own, any more than you could make your way to Hawaii by swimming. But you can still go, because he has taken care of everything. He's bought your ticket, and it has been fully paid for. He's reserved a beautiful space just for you. He's set your place at the table, and he has given you a permanent place in his great heart.

Still, in the end, only you can decide whether you want to go.

He wants you to come. He'll keep inviting you, again and again. But he has given you free will. Ultimately, whatever you choose, he loves you enough to respect your decision.

You already know the rest of Ellen's story. While we were at the Painted Church asking the Lord to love on her, he was busy doing just that. Eventually, she said "Yes" to him and got connected to Love itself. In time, she reconnected with us as well. And I'm so glad!

Looking back on the moment when she finally met the Lord, Ellen says: "I remember thinking, 'This is how God is.' I may have thought I had left my family behind, but God kept coming after me. He kept sending people, and they kept knocking... But it was really God who kept saying, 'Come.' And he gave me the time I needed, till I was ready. After that, it was all about his love."

Jesus paid the full price for all of us, even though it was more terrible than we can dare to imagine. He did that willingly, purposefully, even joyfully. He sought a very great prize, and to him, the end justified the means.

The means was the Cross. Two thousand years ago, God himself laid aside his God-nature. He put skin on and did what we could never do. He lived as a human—but unlike the rest of us, he lived a perfect, sinless life. He personally paid the full penalty for all of our brokenness and sin.

And the end he sought? He saw us as healed and whole, and fully restored to a right relationship with Father God. He saw us living in love and living in glory. He shared his full inheritance rights with us, so that we too can live as Sons and Daughters of the Most High.

That's what he wants for Ellen, and for the rest of our family. It's what he wants for you. [128]

What about you?
God loves you more than you can possibly imagine.
He's calling to you as well.
Will you say, "Yes?"

If you don't know him yet... is this your moment?

Jesus, I'm a sinner and I need a Savior. I don't want to depend on my own goodness anymore. You're so much more than I am, and you've already done what I could never do. I accept your sacrifice on my behalf, and I accept your love. Will you save me and make me alive in you? Thank you, Lord!

If you do know him, he's inviting you even deeper into his love.

Jesus, thank you for loving me like that! I want to know you even better. I want to be so saturated with your love that it fills me up and spills out onto the world around me. From now on, I'm going to ask and keep asking: "Come again! More, Lord!"

Jesus is going to be throwing a huge party in Heaven one day. It's going to be the mother of all parties. He's busy getting everything ready, and he's inviting all of us to come.

I hope to see you there!

Living in the YES!

BONUS MATERIAL:

In Their

Own Words

*Laura*

Wouldn't you like to hear more from the people who shared their stories with us? I think they're all real-life champions: ordinary, everyday people who faced terrible challenges and wrenching pain...and kept going. They're all people who found God's " more" because they would not be defined by crisis or tragedy. They're trailblazers, showing the way to rest of us. We can all live like this! Being connected to God, living in response to him. Living in his YES.

If you're facing a challenge right now, or if you feel stuck, please be comforted. Each of us knows what that feels like. Every person I interviewed was really open about the pain they suffered, and the disappointments they faced. But all of us would encourage you to keep going. Nothing is stronger than God's amazing love for you. He is with you. He wants to empower you so that you, too, discover that you truly are an overcomer.

To my contributors: It's not easy to share this way with a bunch of strangers. From the bottom of my heart, guys, THANK YOU. You've shown the rest us what is possible. I, for one, want to live boldly out of the truth that you learned.

To my readers: Here is the rest of the story.

Living in the YES!

Laura's Story

On March 17, 2017, God miraculously healed me of a traumatic brain injury. Then (we think) he sent an angel to tell us about it. But that's really just part of my story. For a lot of my adult life, my family and I were at the top of everybody's prayer list, because so many things had gone wrong. I was really the unlikeliest person in the world to write a book called *Living in the Yes*. But then God got involved. Now, pretty much everyone in my family has become a walking miracle. We're like the poster children for how good God is. He's just so amazing.

Let me begin at the beginning.

Bob and I both grew up in the South, and we met and married when we were in our mid-twenties. We had two great kids: Alex, who was utterly fearless, and Michael, who our friends called "Bam-Bam" after the "Flintstones" kid because he was big, strong, blond, and full of mischief. Then we adopted Ellen from a Russian orphanage. She was twelve at the time. Also, we've hosted several wonderful exchange students from all over the world, for a year each— Marina, Lola, Anna, Mateus, and Young—plus Frauke, who we got to know while she stayed with Bob's sister.

Somewhere in there, the challenges started appearing.

When Alex was maybe eighteen months old, he fell headfirst off the top level of a playground structure and landed on his head. When the babysitter got to him, he wasn't breathing, wasn't moving, and didn't have a heartbeat. He was resuscitated on the scene and rushed to the hospital, where the neurologist told us he would be fine. But I remember the look in the doctor's eyes as he said, "I can't explain how your son survived this fall." Later, I found out that my Mom had been praying intensely for everyone in our extended family for several weeks, because she'd had a strong sense that one of us was in terrible danger.

Then when we adopted Ellen, we quickly found out that we were not equipped to handle her level of pain and mistrust. And about the same time she came into our world, we were told that Michael was autistic. Life was very chaotic for him. He was smart, but he was easily overwhelmed. He'd fall apart and be unable to calm down, and that happened on a daily basis. He had trouble making friends, which was wrenching, and he was persecuted, bullied. His sunny personality got submerged in all of his trouble, and it was such a loss.

The next seven years were so difficult. Ellen hurt. Michael hurt. The rest of us hurt. Every day, I would ask God, "Please hold on to me, because I don't think I have the strength to hold on to you." When Ellen graduated from high school, she left home and said we'd probably never see her again, and we thought our hearts would break. Back home, Michael was in sixth grade, and he was having a really tough time. Two or three times a week, we'd have to check him out of school before lunchtime because he couldn't cope anymore. The doctors said he would never be able to graduate from high school, because his disabilities were so severe.

But about that time, we started going to a church that really believed God answers prayer, and the whole church started praying for a miracle. They prayed for Michael, they prayed for Ellen, and they prayed for the rest of us. First off, Michael started making little improvements, doing things that the doctors couldn't account for; and we kept praying.

Then we heard from Ellen. While she was living in another state, she'd had a radical encounter with Jesus. It's like that huge hole in her heart had been filled. We couldn't explain it, and she couldn't either. We could only be amazed at what God had done! We started connecting with each other in a different way.

Michael kept slowly, gradually getting better, and he was able to finish high school. Then when he was nineteen, we went to a Global Awakening Conference in Orlando. Bill Johnson said he believed that God wanted to heal learning disabilities, and the people around us started praying for Michael. Soon he started screaming, "It's gone! It's gone! All the noise in my head! All my life I've heard about the peace of God, but now I understand it for the first time!" He was completely healed. His life literally changed overnight.

Remember how I told you that everyone in my family is a walking miracle? Now you know about all my kids. Here's what happened to my husband Bob: his appendix ruptured, and when he went to the hospital ER, they missed it and they sent him home, untreated. Four days later he collapsed and was rushed to surgery. By that point, saving him was a pretty close thing. But our whole church was praying again, and he actually healed up better and faster than anyone thought possible.

Along the way, we faced one crisis after another: financial, health-related, emotional, relational, you name it. Our neighbor was stabbed by a stalker and came to our door asking for help, looking like a bloody mess. We both lost our jobs. Our house was infested with mold, and it took us a couple of years and a ridiculous amount of money to really fix the problem. Lots of things like that. As I said, we were at the top of everybody's prayer list most of the time.

But we'd also seen God show up, again and again. So when I was in a head-on collision and got a traumatic brain injury, I sort of expected to be healed right away. That didn't happen.

I was what they called "functional," but life was really hard for me. The doctor could see on the EEG that my brain didn't light up right in the front and on the left, and all my symptoms lined up with that injury. At first I couldn't understand what anybody said to me unless they talked very s-l-o-w-l-y. I could read the words on a page out loud, but I didn't have any idea what they meant. I had to use my fingers to add "3+4," even though I'd studied calculus. And ordinary noise was overwhelming! I literally had to run away from my own dinner table if two people started talking at the same time, or else I'd be curled up on the floor in a fetal position, screaming, because of the pain in my head.

I couldn't think, couldn't cope, couldn't make any decisions at all. I struggled to remember things. I worked with doctors and therapists and computer programs for several hours a day, trying to get better. And I did get some improvement, just not as much as anybody had hoped for.

I had thought I was a person of faith, but my faith was no match for a crisis of this magnitude. I was scared, and to cover it up, I actually became pretty annoyed with God. "Why aren't you healing me?" I demanded. "I know you could do that. I'm Michael's mother."

That's when the Lord came and spoke to my heart in his still small voice. He told me that I had a much worse problem than the brain injury, and I had done it all by myself. He told me that I didn't really believe I was lovable. I didn't trust other people, and I didn't trust him, either. I had become a controlling overachiever, because I was so afraid of life being out of control. "I know you," he said. "If I heal you right now, you'll go back to living the way you were living before, and that isn't nearly good enough. I want more for you than you want for yourself. Will you trust me?"

And I said, "Yes."

Smartest thing I ever did. I highly recommend saying "Yes" to God.

The next three years became quite an adventure. It was hard to go out in public, because I couldn't cope with the noise. I couldn't go to parties with friends. I couldn't even go to the family Thanksgiving dinner, unless I sat outside and people came to see me one or two at a time. After about an hour of that, I'd go home and sleep for the rest of the day because I was exhausted. Life was just really, really hard. I suffered horribly, for years, and so did everyone who cared about me.

I had to depend on God in order to survive, every single day. I couldn't make any decisions at all. If Bob asked, "Would you like chicken or beef for dinner?" I would burst into tears, because I didn't know. I was so helpless. I had to ask God about everything. I was shocked when I found out that he'd been talking to me all along, way more than I ever knew. I just hadn't been listening. Now I started listening, and the Lord helped me with everything. I started learning about a different way to live, actually being connected to him in real time.

When did things start to change for you?

One day the neuropsychologist got mad at me. "You're not being realistic," she said. "If you could get better by trying hard enough, you'd be better by now. It's just not possible. You're going to have to face the facts. This is what your life is going to look like from now on."

I got mad right back at her. "You don't understand," I told her. "I'm not a private person, I'm a Christian. I'm here at the will and pleasure of Almighty God. I may not understand what's happening in my life, but he does. He has a plan for my life, and I'm gonna trust him until he sees fit to tell me about it. In the meantime, I'm going to do the best I can, and he's gonna walk it out with me. And anyway, I don't believe he's going to leave me like this. One day he's going to come for me. So with his help, I'm going to get up every morning, if it's every day till the day I die, and ask, 'Is today the day that you come for me? If that's not gonna happen today, will you help me?'"

Something about that moment was a turning point for me. It was about that time when I started seeing the waterfall of God's YES, in my mind's eye, and when God asked me to write a book.

What were you learning in those moments?

First of all, God didn't set me up to have the accident—that wasn't his doing—but he did set me up to survive and to succeed. We'd been going to this great church for several years, and they'd been building life and truth and encouragement into me for a while. That strengthened me. It helped me to go through this crisis differently.

After the accident, I felt so helpless and useless. That's when I found out that God didn't just value me because I was "useful." He saw me as valuable, whether I was useful or not. Experiencing that kind of love was a game changer for me.

Especially since the accident, I'd started opening my heart to let God in deeper. I spent a lot of time listening to worship music, praying—which is basically like conversation for me—and soaking in God's presence. My brain could be screaming in agony, which happened pretty much every day, but I could get to peace when I came into his presence.

I couldn't do very much, but I found out that I could still love people. I could listen to them and talk to them, as long as they didn't talk too fast and there wasn't any background noise. I could pray for them, and I got really excited when they got a breakthrough. So I started doing that as much as I could.

Tell us about the night you got healed.

Bob and I went to Birmingham to hear our friend Paul Martini speak at a Christian conference. The Lord whispered some things to me about a young man I didn't know, and I told the guy what I'd heard from God. He and I both got pretty excited, and I said, "Let's pray about that." That's when it happened. I was expecting God to show up for this guy, right? And he did, in a really big way.

The friends who were with us said they watched this massive wave of energy pass through my body, through my hands, into the hands

231

of the guy I was praying for, and it looked like his feet lifted off the ground. I started shaking like I'd been electrocuted, and Bob had to help me to one of the seats in the back of the room.

Now, here's where it gets funny. For over three years, I hadn't been able to take part in church worship without noise-canceling headphones, because I couldn't cope with the noise, and that had been getting worse. I'd actually started standing outside in the parking lot till worship was over. But this night, I was just sitting in the back of the room, shaking like an idiot and crying my eyes out. I'd never left the room, which was IMPOSSIBLE for me, yet I didn't even notice!

When the meeting was over, Bob carried me to the front because I obviously needed some kind of help. A friendly-looking young man came over and said, "You're looking for somebody to pray for you," and I nodded. Not that you could have noticed the nod. I was still shaking like a leaf from head to toe, so the nod just added to the general shake.

The guy smiled and said, "Don't you realize? You don't need anybody to pray for you. Jesus himself has already come. He's already done that which you've been asking for, for so long." Then he left. It took me about ten seconds to take all of that in. Then I asked Bob to go find the guy and bring him back ... but Bob said he was nowhere to be found.

And here's where it gets strange. The guy I saw was average height, maybe about 5'10". He had curly, shoulder-length dark blond hair, and he mostly looked safe and friendly. But the guy Bob saw? He was at least 6'7" with white-blond dreadlocks. Bob said he was massive and slightly terrifying. You figure that one out for yourself.

That's when I realized something had happened, and I was different.

Were all your symptoms healed completely?

Yes, completely, from that first moment on! It was just amazing. My horrible sensitivity to noise had vanished entirely. I could remember things that had been lost to me for over three years. All my MBA skills had come back. I could think again. I could plan. I could do things that were creative. I could do everyday life and have fun—go out for coffee with friends, go to a noisy restaurant with Bob and talk about things. God gave me back my life.

If you could have a do-over, would you still get in the car that day?

Wow. That's a tough question to answer, because choosing to sign up for that degree of pain and misery would be pretty hard. But if I could go back in time, and then keep living the way I used to live before? I would never. What God has given me is so much more, so much better, than any kind of life I would have had otherwise.

Where are all of you now?

Well, I'm obviously healed, and writing and sharing my story are my huge passions. Bob works with a copier company and he talks to people all over the world, and we're both really involved in our local church. We're traveling more.

Ellen is a preschool teacher. She's actually one of the kindest, most relational people I know, and she's an amazing Mom. Alex is an Air

Force Officer who loves to play rugby, travel, and experience adventures. And remember Michael? The little kid they said couldn't graduate from high school? He REALLY isn't autistic anymore. He graduated from Georgia Tech, which is a worldclass university, with honors. Now he lives in another state. He's a successful computer programmer, he's writing a book, and he's really involved with friends and life. All the things they thought he couldn't do are a part of his life now.

I say all of that to tell you: pray for everybody you care about. God loves your whole family even more than you do, and he wants to answer your prayers for them. Co-labor with him to call his Kingdom down.

Really, for the family who was always at the top of everyone's prayer list? I guess that it wasn't such a bad place to be, because God has accomplished more and answered more prayers than I ever could have dreamed of. Of course we still have challenges, and some of them are big ones. We're all still working on stuff. We're all still growing. But I am so grateful, so very grateful.

What would you say to someone who is facing a hopeless situation?

I know what that feels like! Hopeless, helpless, terrified, disappointed, depressed. Can't get better. Won't get better. Multiple crisis situations, piled on top of one another, every single day for years. I know how much it hurts, and I'm sorry. But you don't have to stay there, once you really learn how much God loves you. He will help you. Your life is a gift to be enjoyed and an adventure to be lived! Don't let fear take that away.

Is your situation bigger than your faith? I've been there, too. Stop relying so much on "your" faith. Start relying on God's faithfulness, instead. He's absolutely reliable. No matter what anybody says, no matter what kind of impossible situation you're facing, you turn to God, and you keep turning to him. There's really NOTHING that he can't do.

Lean on him, every single day. Learn how to access his presence. Find a Bible translation that speaks to you, and then drink in his Word. Spend time with other believers who will encourage you. Get your heart healed. Pound on the doors of heaven, asking for miracles. It was especially huge for me to find out what happens when a whole community prays together with faith, when they keep praying and don't give up.

It all comes down to Jesus. He loves you and he's going to be right there with you, no matter what. He's not just "the" healer. He is MY healer, and he wants to be YOUR healer as well. The miracles I've seen, the way I've learned how to live connected to God? I'm convinced: that's the sort of life that is available to every Christian. He wants all of us to know him like that.

Jo's Story

The day I died and met Jesus changed everything.

For six years, I'd been living with excruciating pain from crushed pudendal [pelvic] nerves. I'd already had so many failed surgeries, and I was taking very high doses of narcotics just to survive. This time, the surgeon didn't properly suture the nerve canal. He'd also accidentally nicked my femoral artery, and I was bleeding out. There I was, back in my hospital room, and I knew that something was terribly wrong. With every heartbeat I could feel this gush of warmth rushing out of my body: another gush, and another gush, and another gush, again and again and again. It felt like all my strength was draining away, and I could feel the breath going out of my body.

By the time my sisters got the attention of the medical staff—we were in a foreign country and they weren't very responsive—it was really too late. When they rushed me to the operating room, it was absolute chaos. They couldn't start the anesthetic for emergency surgery. All my veins had collapsed because I'd lost so much blood. They started to move me, and the pain was unbelievable. I knew this was the end. Inside my body there was this primal scream—I knew it was like a last breath—and then there was no more.

It was so weird! One second, I was there in my body, and then I wasn't. I was all the way up at the top of the surgical suite, looking down. Once they'd moved my body, you could see how much blood I'd lost, and there was this unbelievable, bloody mess. More nurses were coming in, and they were covering their mouths, going, *Oh, no*. One male nurse was absolutely in tears. They kept trying to find a pulse and they were like, oh my gosh, oh my gosh. For me, though, it was wonderful. To have absolutely no pain, for the first time in so many years, I was elated. I was in shock, like, Look! I'm free! I decided that I didn't want to look down anymore because it was really gross.

It seemed to me like I waited for a while... and then God came for me.

His glory was so enormous. I was completely overwhelmed by his presence. To experience the majesty of the Father, the feeling is indescribable. It's like nothing else. Maybe there are some words on the planet that would describe it, but I don't know any in English. I wanted to bow, but I didn't have a body, so I couldn't figure out how to do that. I wanted to shrink away. I was so in awe. But there was also this need to open oneself up to the greatest love. God's heart is so magnificent, and it's given out, not just in pieces but the wholeness of it. I was just dumbfounded by the magnitude of his love and the presence of his majesty.

I knew he was my Father, he was my savior, he was my lover, he was my best friend. I knew all of that, in emotion as well as mind as well as heart. I knew it all the way through me. And then, when you're with the Lord there's this complete absence of any fear or doubt. There's no way to explain what that feels like, because on some level, the world has fear everywhere. It's a knowing that you know that you know, that everything is true. Everything in the Bible is true. Everything you can know about God, and more than you can know, it's manifest and it's right there. And I'm like, *what?* I was in shock, awestruck, and completely overwhelmed.

Then he spoke, and his voice was so huge. It went into me and all over me and all around me. It simply filled everything. I don't know what substance a spirit is made of, but it felt like his voice penetrated everything about me, all the way down to a molecular level. It was both awe-inspiring and terrifying, yet so loving. I wasn't afraid. My human brain just couldn't comprehend.

I didn't have any doubt at all that I was created by this amazing God, for this amazing God, and that I would be with this amazing God forever. I had this absolute assurance. It was like a feeling and a knowing that you could never get on the earth. I just loved him, more than I knew it was possible to love. And all I wanted to do was to be with him, and I never wanted to leave him.

And he said: "I have seen your suffering, Child, and I know full well your pain." I'll never forget it! Those words were just seared into me. It's the most amazing thing, you know? Like, *oh my gosh, he knows me.*

He said, "You can go with me now or you can stay, for the prayers of the Saints have given you a choice." And I'm like, *What? Prayers don't give people choices.* Then I'm actually thinking, *God, are you crazy? There's no way I'm going down there again. Who would do that?*

And the next thing, I can see my son. It's not like I'm seeing a video or a picture or a hologram, it's like I actually was where he was. I see his blond, blond hair and those huge blue eyes, and he's looking at me and smiling. I can see my husband in the distance, as well. And I'm mesmerized, looking at my child. I'm thinking: he's so beautiful, and he is God's greatest gift to me. Then I think about how much trauma my husband and my son have already been through, with all my pain and all the surgeries, and I don't say anything, but I think: *if I leave, it's gonna be more than they can bear.*

Then the Lord said to me, "It is as you wish, Child." And I thought, *Wait. Did I wish that?* I didn't understand it then, but I understand it now. Love is a choice. It's a power, it's a force, and it propels things into being, spiritually. And I chose to love.

Then my spirit started to descend back down into the room, and God was coming down with me. He was around me, in me, through me. He warned me, "You will know much pain," and immediately I wanted to backtrack and change my mind, but love had already chosen. He was whispering to me, assuring me, like a father to a child. "Don't be afraid, no matter what. Don't be afraid, don't be afraid, don't be afraid. I will never fail you. I'm not going anywhere. I'm never going to leave you. I'm never going to forsake you. I'm going to be with you, minute by minute." And he said other things as well. Some of them were for me alone, and I don't talk about those.

Then, right before I came back into my body, it's like fear came off the room onto me. I don't know how to describe it. And the last words the Lord had said to me, he kept repeating them. It was so loud inside of me. I can hear his voice like it was yesterday: "Minute by minute."

Then, *wham!* I slam into my body, and it feels like ten million needles or shards of glass are jammed into me all at the same time, but that's over very quickly. After that, I'm in the same unbearable pain that I had when they wheeled me into the operating room. Just at that very moment they jam a huge needle into my spine with no anesthetic, and I pass out.

Later, when I was back in my hospital room, I saw Jesus. He wasn't there in physical form; my eyes were closed. I saw his face, I saw his eyes. I had no words, no dialogue with him, just to see the beauty of his eyes. He was weeping over me, and I knew that he loved me. Remembering it now makes me weep. After that, while I was in that hospital room, I couldn't function at all. I just kept seeing Jesus' face, I kept hearing the Father's voice, and all I could do was relive every moment I'd had, up on the ceiling.

I needed another emergency surgery the next day. Long story short, it was weeks before I could go back home, and months before I could function at all. Eventually I had a kind of a life, still surviving on high doses of narcotics. In time, I got a part-time job at a church. I couldn't sit, but I'd be kneeling on the floor on my knees, typing. I couldn't really do much with husband or my son, and that was the hardest part. All in all, I had basically fifteen years of excruciating pain, and thirteen surgeries—none of which helped me all that much—before I was healed.

Tell me about that.

Well, I'd been going to a church that didn't really believe in divine healing, but I started hearing people talk about how God still heals today, so I was checking it out. I read a lot of books by Randy Clark and Bill Johnson. And I felt like the Lord told me to go to Randy's big conference, which was in Orlando that year, in August 2013.

While I was there at the conference, maybe a hundred people had prayed for me, and I had been blasted by the power of God. I was experiencing such levels of his glory, and I was having encounters with his presence, but I wasn't any better. In fact, I had been moving

240

around a lot, so now I was in really, really difficult pain. We had spread out blankets on the floor in the back of the room, where I could either lay down or kneel, and I had a little tribe of people around me. And I was resigned to the fact that God wasn't going to heal me.

Then—it's only about two hours before the conference ends—I see this big man coming towards me. He has white hair and he's really tall, and his name tag says "Richard." In a heavy Texas accent, he says, "Hey, what's your story?"

Now, I was really annoyed. I'd had so much prayer that week, and I didn't want to have to stand up anymore, and I didn't want anyone else to pray for me. But I didn't want to be rude, either, so I just said, "I'm a chronic pain patient. I've had a lot of surgeries, and I've been this way for a really long time. It's okay. I'm fine."

Well, he doesn't take the hint. He goes, "Well, is it all right if I pray for you?" and I answer, "I guess." So I stand up, and he says, "I bless you" or something like that. I get thrown backwards by the power of God, and my friends catch me and let me down onto the floor. I was completely out of it for, like, fifteen minutes, and my body was shaking all over from the power of God, but when I came to, I wasn't any better. So when I saw him coming back, I said, "Oh, no." I was flat-out, full-blown irritated. I put my hand up, like I was telling him to back off. I really didn't want him to pray for me anymore, and I told him so.

That's when Richard yells, "NO!" really loud. It kind of freaked me out. And he goes: "God healed me. He healed my wife. He healed my son. And now he's gonna heal YOU!" Then he sits in a chair. He takes my face in his hands—remember, I'm kneeling because it hurts so much to stand up—and he tells me to keep looking into his eyes, no matter what. He says that he binds the powers of darkness. Then he starts telling me all sorts of things: "You have difficulty swallowing. At night you have to sleep propped up, and you believe you can't eat anything." He went on and on, telling me one thing after another about my physical condition, and all of them were true. Some of those things, even my husband didn't know at the time. And the Holy Spirit was on me, and that's making me shake like crazy, and I'm sobbing.

Next Richard says that I need to renounce all the lies I've believed. These were things that nobody knew but me and God, but Richard knew: *I've never really been forgiven for all the wild stuff I did in my teens and twenties. I'm rejected. I'm worthless. I have always been a problem to my Father. I'm not lovable.* It went on and on, and he had me break my agreement with all of those things.

Then he told me the deepest secret of all: that I was mad at God. By this point, I'm sobbing, Richard is sobbing, and everyone else is sobbing. Richard is looking at me, and I see Jesus in his eyes. And as I say, "I'm sorry, God. Forgive me for judging you and making this your fault," he says the most wonderful words: "You are forgiven." As he does, it feels like I've been carrying a whole truckload of weight on my shoulders, ever since my childhood, and suddenly it lifts, and it's completely gone.

"You are forgiven." You know, as Christians we don't realize the power of those words. People need to hear, audibly hear, those words, and God says in the New Testament that as Kingdom priests, we're allowed to say them. I'm so glad Richard knew that.

Then he had me tell a bunch of evil spirits to go, the spirit of infirmity, the spirit of death, the spirit of trauma. He told them to go, as well. And that time, when he prayed for me, I was healed! He said to get up and do something I couldn't do, and that's when I realized that I could lift my right leg for the first time in years. He and my friend Monica half-dragged and half-carried me up to the front, because I was staggering under the power of God, and I got to tell everyone what had just happened to me. As I did, the whole room erupted in praise, and a whole lot of other people got healed of nerve damage on the spot. From that point on, all the physical symptoms were completely gone. Praise God!

Now I can look back at those old videos and I just sob. I can hardly recognize myself, because of how tormented I was. God has brought me so far. I'm nowhere near the person I was when I was healed, on August 16, 2013. And I hope, if I talk to you again in five years, I'll be completely different again. Glory to glory to glory! I want to be in this process till I walk off the Earth.

What has all of this taught you about the heart of God?

It's unfathomable. It's immeasurable. We now know of two trillion galaxies, and God says he knows every one of those stars by name. How about that? There's more of his love than you could ever imagine. There's more love he has for you, and there's more love he wants to pour through you. His love is a catalytic force that changes us. It can change the structure of a whole nation. We don't understand it. You can't comprehend the magnitude of the Father's

243

love. To be in his presence, I felt like: *nothing could ever compare to this*. To experience being accepted and loved that much. To know I was that approved of, that loved, that adored by this God who is so enormous, gave me a perspective I'd never had before. It gave me the courage to face what was ahead. God changed everything.

What did you learn about yourself?

You know, Richard was right. All those years, even after I'd come back from death, I didn't really think God was gonna heal me. I didn't believe I deserved it. Deep, deep down at the core of my being, I thought I deserved to suffer as a punishment for the way I'd lived my life in my teens and twenties. I thought what a lot of Christians think, that God is sovereign, and he could heal me if he wanted to. I figured he didn't want to. Looking back, though, it wasn't that God had a problem with me. It's more like I had a problem with me. I didn't really understand forgiveness. I didn't understand all that Jesus had actually paid for. I didn't understand the power of agreement. I'm so glad I know better now.

Life now is incredibly awesome. God is so good! I wake up every day and just go, Thank you! It feels amazing to have no issues in my body. This morning while I was running, the kids at the elementary school knocked their ball over a really high fence. I trotted all the way around the schoolyard to give it back to them, and they were racing with me, and we were all laughing. It just amazes me every day.

After I was healed, I went to seminary for Christian life coaching and training teams. Now I have a ministry called Agape Freedom Fighters. We go all over the world. I love showing people what it's like to be a family on a mission, not just a bunch of people who go to

244

church together. We talk about the Biblical basis for healing, and how to have a love affair with Jesus instead of only having head knowledge about him. We want to help ordinary people know how to go out and do this stuff—but not as a project. Never as a project. People aren't projects. They just need to be loved.

What would you say to someone who has been sick for a long time?

First of all, get healed up internally. I'm talking about your emotions. Isaiah 61 is a great framework for examining this stuff. It says Jesus came to bind up the brokenhearted. He sets the captives free and releases those who are imprisoned. Where are you brokenhearted? Where in your heart or your mind are you held captive? Has the enemy imprisoned you, and you don't even realize it, by the words people have spoken over you or the things you've agreed with? I would let Jesus encounter me in those ways, and I would get a trained healing minister to help.

I would go through and write yourself a whole thing about God's healing promises, and about what Jesus did. Then read it and declare it again and again. I would keep reminding myself about the testimonies of what God has done for me, and what he's done for others, over the years. I would go through Ephesians, and Romans, and write down: who does God say that you are? Because when you've been sick, the way you think about yourself probably isn't the true identity of a born-again Christian. Declare the truth over yourself –not in a rote, religious kind of way, but inviting the truth into your mind, body, soul. Let God encounter all those things in you that need to be healed.

I do want to clarify, by the way, that I don't believe God ever causes pain. He warned me that I would know pain, but that wasn't because he was causing it. I just think the enemy had a field day with my life.

Don't deny your pain, because that doesn't help anyone. If you need medical care, get it. If you need medications, use them. Continue to contend and press in for your healing. Continually focus on who Jesus is, and never lose sight of that. And when you start to stumble, get yourself around like-minded believers who can pray for you and hold you up. And get as much prayer as you possibly can. Pray and keep praying! And stand fearless before the Lord. If you're brokenhearted because you have a setback, he doesn't ever leave you. He's still with you.

When you came back, you were still in a lot of pain, but God had told you that he would be with you minute by minute. What did that look like?

When you're in a situation like that, you have to draw closer to God. It's an attitude of turning towards God and leaning on him. You have to know who Christ is. He is our healing, our freedom. He's our identity, our authority, our power. In all things he is perfect love. He is the Person of Truth, the Prince of Peace. When things happen, when thoughts come to my mind that come against that understanding of who Christ is, I don't permit myself to think about them. I actively turn away from them. I can only understand what is true in relation to perfect Truth. You keep turning towards God, minute by minute, and you choose to rely on the fact that he's going to be all those things for you. You ask him for help.

Who is Jesus? Who did he say that I am? Don't deny your pain, but discipline your thought life and choose to focus on that truth. Look up Second Corinthians 10:5, look up Philippians 4:8, that's what this is all about. Keep your mind active, but it needs to be activity according to God's Kingdom rather than the world.

You'll have to practice. When your mind gets rooted in garbage thinking, it's like driving a truck down a dirt road in the same ruts, over and over. You have to practice thinking about different things. That's how you create new neural pathways. That's not only scriptural. Modern medical research supports it as well.

Most importantly, remember how much you're accepted and loved by this God who is so enormous. Nothing in your life can stop that from being true. No matter what you're facing, you'll only be able to make sense of it if you start by knowing how much he loves you.

What would you say to someone whose friend is sick?

Stop giving so much advice! Your friend or loved one doesn't need more advice; what they need is more of your listening and more of your love. Don't send them ten million Scriptures they need to read or ten million songs they need to hear. Send one. Don't tell them other people are worse off than they are, and certainly don't tell them that nobody else is suffering as much as they are. Neither of those things helps.

Ask the Lord for a word that will encourage your friend today. And ask your friend: What do you need the most? What will help you right now? And I will guarantee you that if they're in pain, many times they'll say they just want you to come spend time with them and not say anything. The power of silence is so underrated, the power of just being there.

Finally, pray. Speak the Lord's words back to him. Lord, your Word says that everyone you encountered, you healed. Your Word says that the lame walk. Your Word says that the blind saw. Your Word says that you're the same yesterday, today and forever, and your promises are true. Whatever it is. It really messed with my theology when God told me, "The prayers of the saints have given you a choice." But it's in the Bible, in Revelations 8 and other places. Prayers are timeless and they have great power. All the people who were praying for me, I don't think they had any idea what the effect of their prayers was going to be.

What would you say to a person whose loved one died and didn't come back?

Oh, that's the hardest question I get. I know what it's like to lose people I've loved, and it's never easy.

Grief is a process. Let the Holy Spirit take you through the process. You'll think you're through it, and you're not. Get prayer, and get support—not from someone who wants to give you advice, but from someone who will sit with you, hold your hand, and let you cry. And it's normal to have anger towards God for someone being taken from you. But let God lead you through the process of forgiving even him.

Having encountered God, there's one thing I know for sure. No matter how much they loved you, your loved one doesn't want to be back here. They're being celebrated, and they're celebrating! They're home and they're happy and they're free. For me, even for that short time, being with God, being loved like that, was like truly being home. I never wanted to leave him, and I couldn't bear the idea of being apart from him. If I had stayed with him even a little bit longer, or experienced more of his presence, could I have chosen to come back? I don't know.

And here's another thing: You don't have to remember your loved one as old, or sick, or suffering, because they're definitely not like that anymore. Ask God to give you revelation of who they are now.

My father just passed away, and I asked God to let me see him without pain. I was expecting to have a dream or something, but in the middle of his celebration of life service, as I was singing Psalm 23, I had an open vision of heaven. I just folded in half and started sobbing. I could see Jesus standing there, and my Dad was with him, but I've never in my life seen my father look like that. He was tormented his whole life. He always had this angry, mean kind of look. He was stubborn and prideful and arrogant, and he held grudges until he died, and a lot of other stuff. But now he looked like he was 30 and there was no more pain, no more suffering, no more torment, and he was smiling at me! And I'm going, oh my gosh, that's a different face. It was incredible. Incredible!

Tell me about your book.

It's called *Minute by Minute,* and it's the story of everything that happened to me. It's an easy read, and there are parts that are humorous because that's my life. If you're dealing with chronic pain or chronic setbacks, or if you're in a long battle, I hope you get it and I pray that it blesses you. It's a story of hope. It's the story of Almighty God, who is timeless, intersecting a moment in time and

249

doing what everybody said was impossible, creating a miracle. Let the power of testimony encounter you, and let it be God's opportunity for healing.

Ian's Story

Four days after our first child was born, my wife Rozanne suddenly developed a blood infection and died. At first, I didn't know what to do. It was so unexpected. I was in shock and I just felt numb. There I was, not only single again, but a single Dad. I think the hardest thing about it was, the one person you want to have by your side when you go through something really hard is the person you just lost. The other thing was the feeling of loss. Not only had I lost my partner, but in a sense it felt like the last three to five years of my life were gone, because I had lost the person who'd shared those experiences.

What did you do?

At first you don't think about tomorrow. You just have to get through today. Of course you have to take the time to grieve. But because I had a new baby to care for, there wasn't too much time for me to be sort of self-indulgent and wallow. I had to figure out who was going to care for her while I went back to work. I had to figure out how to make it through the day. At first, that's all I had the capacity for. Honestly, most of that stage is a blur.

I'm very blessed because for the first several months, my parents and Rozanne's parents flew out and helped care for Abi. Then a couple in our church stepped in and became an ongoing part of our journey in so many ways, lining up childcare, encouraging me, and meeting many practical needs.

In time, another family also stepped in to help. It's really something the Lord orchestrated. Michelle wasn't looking to be a nanny, but she felt ready because of various experiences they had been through as a family. They ended up being so much more than caretakers. Michelle, her husband and her children welcomed Abi into their home and they really just embraced her. Abi got to experience family and siblings, and the continuity of having the same caregiver in her life from the time she was one till the time she was six and a half was really sweet. Michelle and her family were such an important part of our lives.

Was it hard for you to cope as a single Dad?

I think for all parents, that first year is so isolating. You can't do life in exactly the same way you did before. And the world doesn't know what to do with single Dads in general. You don't exactly fit with your single friends and you don't really fit with other families. Honestly, there were so many times I just stayed at home because I didn't have the capacity to cope when things didn't go according to plan. But there were people who made room in their lives for us in ways that weren't necessarily convenient for them, like the people who planned a family vacation and invited us to come along. People who were steadfast and encouraging over the years. That's really special. It's easy to journey with someone for a little bit of time, but it's not easy to journey with them for years and years.

I think it was some time after the first year that I started to think, okay, I have a little more capacity for life. I can move beyond the question of whether I can survive today. Where do I want to invest that? I want to find friendship. I want to take better care of my health, emotionally, physically and spiritually. That was a turning point.

What were the tough questions for you?

In the beginning there's a tendency to ask, "Why did this happen to me? Why didn't the Lord prevent it?" I still don't have a great answer to that. But I quickly realized that knowing it wouldn't get me anywhere. Did Rozanne have a compromised immune system? Did the hospital do something they shouldn't have? I could have known all those answers and I would still be stuck.

But I had a relationship with the Lord. I knew what it was like to feel his presence and to hear from him. The evidence of his presence in my life was overwhelming. There were so many specific moments in my life when he had worked things out, things that were not possible in the natural. That made it so much easier to deal with the times when my emotions tried to take charge. So I already knew, I'm holding on. Even when I don't understand, even when it doesn't make sense to me. His promises, even the ones that seemed like they would never be fulfilled, were just as true as they ever were. He gave me the strength to say, "The Lord is good and he is for my good." My pastor really helped. He told me, give yourself time to grieve. Give yourself time to figure out life. If it takes years, that's fine. There's no rush.

I knew that what had happened wasn't a surprise to God. I came to the point of asking a different kind of question. I'd tell the Lord, "Okay, I don't know why this happened and I don't need to know. But I do need you to tell me: What comes next? How do I go forward from here? The dreams I've had, your promises over my life, how does all of that work now?"

How did your life move forward from there?

Eventually I started to build community and feel like I could begin to enjoy life again. When I realized I was ready to pursue another relationship, that was definitely another turning point. But I had a few relationships that didn't work out. They were plenty of opportunities to think, "This is happening to me and I don't like it! If I was making the plan, I would make it differently." Abi had been without a mom for seven years and clearly the best time for her to get a mom would have been years ago.

In time, I got to the point of saying, "Okay, Lord, whether this works or not, I'm going to be fine." It was only after that, when I finally met Stefanie.

Tell me about that.

We met online. I had a lot of reservations about that process. To me it's very artificial. It's a sort of sanitized experience and it's not grounded in reality. So it was really shocking to meet in person and discover that she had been to my church, and she knew people really well who I knew and trusted. That was kind of a game changer for me. It was the first of many examples of the Lord saying, I've heard your concerns. I got to see Stefanie in some stressful situations and I could see how she handled difficulty. We connected easily, and we became really good friends. It's so amazing how God worked out the details. He had been preparing her for years to be my wife and Abi's mom. As a social worker, she had worked with adoption and blended families, and she had worked with a children's hospice, helping families deal with loss. We've been married now for almost a year, and we couldn't be happier!

At the end of this experience, what things do you know to be true?

God is faithful, so he will do the things he said he will do. He is who he says he is. He will come through. We don't have to understand exactly how. And then Stefanie and I talk about Ephesians 3:20, and how God is able to do immeasurably more than all that we ask or imagine, according to his power at work within us. There are so many different ways he's done that for us. There's such a sweetness in it.

What advice do you have for someone who's going through a crisis?

If it's at all possible, try not to make big decisions in those early stages. Be gracious to yourself, and find other people who will be gracious to you, because there will be bad days when your emotions run away with you. Find community, and keep surrounding yourself with other people instead of becoming isolated. Find purpose in your daily life so you don't end up spending the whole day focusing on how things didn't work out the way you had planned. Know that you will get through it, and when you've survived something like this, other challenging times just won't seem so challenging. And trust that the day will come when you can feel happy again.

Read on to hear more of their story from Ian's wife, Stefanie.

Stefanie's Story

There was a time when it felt like my life was falling apart, and I believed it was all my fault. I'd been married less than a year and it was obvious that we were in trouble. My husband kept telling me, "You're so anxious. You're so insecure. You have a problem and you need to get help."

So I did everything I could. Marriage is a covenant you make, you know? You take that very seriously. I changed jobs so I could have a less demanding schedule. I went to individual counseling and we saw a marriage counselor. My husband's interests had changed, so I tried to make some lifestyle changes like going dancing with him more. But he'd started doing some things I didn't feel comfortable with, drinking a lot, clubbing, other things.

Did it work?

No. I spent the next two years trying to save my marriage, but things between us didn't get any easier. Eventually I found out that he'd developed a sexual addiction. I saw what was on his phone, and what was on his computer, and what was hidden in plain sight in our bank records. I found his online journal and you could see the downhill slide in his life. He'd been seeing another woman, and he'd spent so much money in ways that just shocked me. He'd been lying to me, to a degree that I couldn't even imagine. I still didn't want a divorce. I just wanted him to repent and change, and to fight for our marriage. But I finally realized, just because I kept choosing to love, it didn't mean that my husband was going to make the same choice.

How did you feel?

It was heartbreaking and devastating and gut-wrenching. I had to grieve the death of our marriage. It's a helpless feeling, seeing someone you care about change in front of your eyes like that. At first, I felt such a deep sense of betrayal, and then I felt really angry. As I realized what was actually happening in my marriage, I felt broken and ashamed, like I had done something wrong. I couldn't identify anything I loved about myself. Eventually I realized things weren't going to change and I knew this wasn't the way God designed marriage. When the divorce was final, it was almost a relief. I had a fresh start. What was I going to do? I was able to start dreaming again.

How did you get through that time?

I was going to my counselor and also to a support group for women whose husbands have sexual addictions. I journaled a lot, and I think that's a great way to process your emotions. And I had the sweetest friends and family! None of them had been through a divorce. They didn't know what it was like. But they would call and invite me to hang out. They would say things like, "You're not going to be alone because I'm here with you."

Maybe the most important thing was how much time I spent with God. I'd been a social worker in pediatric hospice situations, which was such an honor, such a special, sacred time. The kids told me what they would see and hear right before they went to heaven, so I knew God was real. I knew I needed him. I spent a lot of time listening to worship music. I spent a lot of time in prayer, even on the days when all I could manage to say was, "Help me, help me."

257

Was anything especially transforming for you?

One life-changing experience was when I went for Sozo [a form of inner healing ministry.] I started learning that I could hear from God, and not just through Bible study or the wisdom of others; I could hear him for myself. Hearing his voice is like hearing a gentle whisper that you know you wouldn't say and you almost want to argue against. There's this quiet truth that you can't deny because of the peace and clarity it brings.

Also, I came to realize how much of my life was tied up in shame. It was all about performance and whether I was good enough. Even with God, I'd think, "This is how I need to behave, these are the rules I need to follow if I want to be acceptable." But God's grace is the antidote to shame, and I craved grace. My old sense of shame got replaced with a sense of, "I'm okay. Lord, I'm seen by you. I don't have to measure our relationship with a scorecard, because you don't. You just love me." I know that's true, because he speaks to my heart and tells me himself, and I feel such peace. I learned that I was valuable, and feeling confident in that was okay, it wasn't a form of pride. I've become so much more secure, knowing that I'm acceptable and I am loved.

Where do you think God was in all of your pain?

I don't think God planned for this to happen, but I do think he loves us enough to give us freedom to choose. He's not like a controlling father, shouting, "Do what I say!" He gives us guidelines that are supposed to help us, but then he allows us to choose for ourselves. In my ex-husband's case, I think he'd had a lot of trauma, things he didn't work through in his own life. And I think he came to the point where he chose not to pursue God anymore. He chose to pursue other things, distractions really, things that made him feel happy in the moment.

Where was God in all of that? He was with me. Psalm 40:1-3 became my lifeline, where it talks about God's promise of lifting us out of the mud and the mire. I had this visual of God, steadying me as I walked along, and that's what did happen.

Now you have a great marriage with Ian. Was that your miracle?

My life with Ian and Abi is such a blessing, and it's way more than I could ask or imagine. But long before I met them, the miracle had already happened. I was already healed and whole. God did that. The healing, the wholeness, that was my miracle.

What would you say to someone who's in a crisis, or who loves someone in a crisis?

If you have a friend who's hurting, take the time to talk to them. It was really hard when I would be around people, say at church, and they knew I was going through a divorce but they would just ignore it. That felt like torture. I didn't need them to say much, but I needed them to say something. A simple, "How are you?" or "I'm so sorry you're going through this," went a long way. I especially treasured the times when people would just listen and give me a chance to talk. I needed them to not judge me, and to not offer unsolicited advice. I just needed the chance to feel heard and understood.

If you're the one who's hurting, be gracious with yourself. You'll have good days, and then you'll have days when you feel sad or angry or insecure. That's a normal part of the process, you just don't have to

259

stay there. I refused to be the person who still had unresolved grief twenty years later because I hadn't dealt with it. Find a counselor, and journal, and find people who love the Lord and who will pray for you. Spend time with friends. Most of all, spend time with the Lord.

Do you have any final thoughts?

I want to acknowledge that this was hard. Even now it can be hard, and I don't want to gloss over that. But it was worth it. I think going through hard times gives you strength and courage. And there's nothing that God won't carry you through. Nothing! No time that he won't stay alongside you. He is not going to abandon you. Even if you feel abandoned, it doesn't mean he's left, it just means that you can't see him right now. I know the Lord as my champion, in a way I couldn't have known if I hadn't gone through what I did. Without that, I wouldn't be where I am today. I would do it again, and I said that long before I met Ian.

I knew the Lord would help me, but I had no idea how intimate the journey was going to be, or that there would be so much freedom in his presence. When you're in the pit of despair he will pick you up. He will. And it will transform you in a way that wouldn't have happened if you just saw it in someone else. It's the most amazing, incredible thing. That's what I would wish for other people, that they could experience this kind of intimacy with God.

"Rachel's" Story*

My life used to revolve around all my activities. It's a vicious cycle that started innocently enough. You're doing, doing, doing, because you want to succeed. I thought doing things for God showed him how much I loved him. If I did more, I thought it would please him more, and then maybe I would feel better about myself. I'd spent my whole life trying to be a "good girl." I was just very busy, trying to lead the model life I thought a good Christian should live. I thought that was how I could earn God's blessing. But I got into this performance mindset. It felt like I didn't ever measure up to my expectations, or to God's. There's always one more thing you need to do. It was such an exhausting way to live.

How did it affect you, living like that?

What I did was never enough, and it was controlling my life. It was controlling my poor children's lives, which were really not all that great. When I walked into the room all I could see was what they lacked, not what was right about them. It resulted in very negative self-talk that started when I woke up and pretty much went on all day. I would not say I was dysfunctional. On the outside, I was functioning quite well. I raised my children and kept my home. I had relationships with friends and things like that; but I lived with a very unhealthy, negative internal conflict for many years.

---

* Not her real name.

I really had a clear sense that God loved me, because he died for me. I knew his love secured an eternal place in heaven. But it did not translate into everyday life. Why would God want to bless me, favor me or answer my prayers? I always felt like I fell short in what I said, what I did, how I looked, anytime I tried to do something.

You keep trying, but you get worn out. Eventually you give up. I thought I'd never do enough to please God. That's when I started having real problems. I turned into a control freak and nobody even wanted to be around me. You think you're free when you're in charge of everything, but that kind of life isn't freedom, it's slavery.

What changed for you?

I woke up one day and realized I was never going to be able to do enough. That's where the Lord began to show me that I could trust in his faithfulness, and my identity journey began. Remember, nothing I did ever felt like it was good enough. Then I found this series of messages on righteousness, and I listened to them over and over. It transformed my life! All the pressure of doing it right, thinking right, speaking it right, believing right, all the pressure was off because I learned that God's favor came simply through my faith in Jesus.

It seems like your life is very different now.

I can't describe enough the way I feel now compared to how I felt then. I learned one simple truth, that God accepts me. I can just focus on who Jesus is, what he accomplished on my behalf, and what he says about me, instead of having to constantly evaluate what I'm doing. Those negative thoughts are always available, but now I know I'm right with God, and I'm fully qualified to live an abundant life.

262

He's not up there taking account of my performance. Now I can just focus on living in that reality.

I can't say that I trust the Lord perfectly. Obviously, we're all growing. But I do not have to be perfect, and I am okay with being in process. There are still days I have to work at it. But I never have to walk away miserable, feeling like I didn't perform. I am not going to beat myself up because I had a rough day.

What does that look like on an everyday basis?

For so much of my life, I lived a very different version of the Willie Nelson song. "I" was always on my mind. How can I look better, how can I live better, how can I eat better, how can I do better? How can I contribute to God's kingdom? This has really freed me to spend more time thinking about how I can be a blessing to other people, because I'm not always trying to fix myself. Now other people are on my mind, helping them see who they are as God's unique creative expression. For them to see their value and worth. It's freed me up to actually live out of a passion that God put in me.

Do you have any advice for someone else who is struggling in this area?

There are so many things I would love to say to someone like that. Give yourself permission to be in process, and lighten up. Take the focus off of trying to fix yourself. Spend time focusing on what has already been done for you, so the Lord can bring you truth and life. The other thing is to get around like-minded people. Your freedom comes when you hear the gospel, but it will happen so much quicker if you find community.

Ellen's Story

I was adopted from Russia when I was twelve. It was exciting, but everything was very different. The food was different, the culture was different. I didn't speak any English. I had to see a lot of doctors and dentists and tutors. I missed Russian food, and the culture and the language. And I missed my old friends. Before, I'd been living in an orphanage. Now, I had a new country, a new language, and a new set of parents.

What were some of the everyday situations you faced?

Well, at first I couldn't express what I needed or wanted, so that was frustrating on both sides. We communicated through books and pictures, or else we would have to call a translator.

And so many little things changed. For example, in the orphanage you had one set of clothes that you would wear all week. Then once a week, they would give you clean clothes. When I came here, I had to learn that I couldn't wear the same thing every day. And at the orphanage, some of my experiences with doctors and dentists had been pretty bad, so I had to get used to going for regular dental checkups and going to the doctor. At first, I would hide food in my room because I was afraid somebody was going to take it away. And of course, I was a teenager. Emotionally and physically, I was going through a lot.

What about the bigger challenges?

Well, school was hard. I was behind, and I didn't really understand the value of an education. That was never imprinted in me from a young age, that it can take you places as you get older. That was like the last thing, if you even thought about it.

Just being part of a family was something that took a while to understand and appreciate. In the orphanage, most of the teachers don't really connect emotionally, and there's only maybe two people that I trusted. You learn to rely on yourself, because nobody else is going to take care of you. You just have to fend for yourself and do the best you can. It's a whole mentality of just trying to survive and, you know, make sure you have something to eat the next day. Make sure the older kids don't take your lunch tomorrow, or anything like that. So trust was hard.

Tell me more about that.

For some people it's a big thing. Like feeling, oh, I don't belong here. And part of that is probably because they feel there's an emptiness. You might have the most wonderful family, but they can't fill that hole, they can't fill that emotional scar. You still might not feel like you belong. And your family is like, "Yes, you do belong here! We love you no matter what!" But you have to be able to believe it. I think God has to work on that.

It was like that for me. My new family said that they loved me. But really trusting my parents and my siblings, that I was in a good place and they wanted the best for me? That took me a long time. You know, letting my family members in and letting them care for me. Really, the whole time I was going to school and living with my parents, I wasn't sure about that. First I had to figure out what healthy trust in a relationship looks like. That takes a while, I think, especially if you've been through trauma.

265

What do you think makes someone trustworthy?

Knowing that they're safe. You can go to that person and they won't judge you, if you share something. Being consistent with what they say, and seeing that they follow through with their behavior. I don't think trust should just be thrown out there. It's a privilege and a choice. You learn how much you can trust people over time. Some friends, you can only make small talk. You can't really have deep conversations with them. Other friends you can share stuff with, because you've learned that you can trust them.

When did things start to change for you?

It was after I moved away from home. I was living in Texas, and someone invited me to church. I didn't go, but they kept inviting me. Eventually I did go with them. And I didn't go to the altar the first time I went to church ... but I remember the day that I did decide to go. That's when it was *my* decision to say, "Okay, Jesus, I'm going to follow you," versus "Okay, I'm going to church with my family because that's what *they* are doing." There wasn't any huge change at first, I just felt such a sense of peace. From there, I started thinking differently and doing things differently, but it took a little bit of time.

That first night, I remember thinking, "This is how God is." You know, I thought I'd left my family behind, but I hadn't gotten away from God. He just kept coming after me. He kept sending people, and they kept knocking on my door, saying, "Come on! We would love to have you at church!" I realized that this situation was more than me, running into some very persistent people. It was really God himself who was persistent. He kept saying, "Come, come." And then he gave me the time I needed, till I was ready.

266

Later on, I had a healing moment. I think it was Rob Rufus who came to speak. He was talking about grace and forgiveness, and what they really mean. I hadn't come with any type of intention—like, oh, I'm gonna let something go. But I guess I had an encounter with God. All of a sudden I didn't have that burden, that feeling of, "Oh, I'm an orphan, poor me," that type of victim thing, anymore. It was like a weight just lifted off of me. And now I know—once, I *was* an orphan. A lot of bad things *did* happen. But that's all in the past. I don't have that feeling anymore. Now, I still have things to work on, but I don't have the same issues that I did when I first came. That part of my brain has been rewired, I think, by the Lord.

I think the big thing for me, in order to believe that God loves me? It was when I became a Mom. I had these little "aha" moments with God, where I thought, "I get it now." Loving my daughter helped me understand how God loves me.

Do you have any advice for someone who struggles with trust?

You have to let God heal those wounds. Some of the deeper ones take longer to heal, but that depends on if you're willing to let it go. If you still want to hold on, you probably won't heal for a long time.

I think the first step is learning to trust God. You know, when you decide to become a believer, you're believing and trusting that Jesus was here, and he did die on the cross for my sins. You have to believe that. And then you have to trust your emotions to God. He has to come and do adjustments on them, kind of like a chiropractor. From there it kind of branches out, and you learn how to trust other people. God will give you wisdom in that area.

Living in the YES!

The Bible says that God wants to adopt every one of us into his family. Based on your experience with adoption, do you have any thoughts about that?

Adoption is someone taking you in and choosing to love you. It's a big gift, to find people who are willing to do that. And you know, God is the same way. He'll adopt anyone! We know that. He chooses us, and he loves us, no matter what.

But we have to choose, too, and it's not always easy. Hard things can happen. Sometimes life is very difficult. It's a choice, do you want to get up every day? Are you going to trust, or are you going to be miserable? Are you gonna forgive—and it might take a little bit of time—or are you gonna be miserable? And if you don't forgive, it really is hurting you. The other person doesn't care, they're not even thinking about you. You're the one that's suffering. I think a lot of life is a choice.

God says, "I will give you peace." But what is that like? How do we feel peace in the bad times, when we're stressed? When we remember bad things that happened, or when bad things are happening now? That's when I spend time with the Lord and ask him to encourage me. And I think, "I'm gonna choose joy. I'm not gonna let people put me down, and I'm not gonna let situations get me down. I choose to be in a good mood." God says that he's always with us, and I choose to trust that. I think that's what it means to have a childlike faith.

Humanly it would not be possible, just relying on your emotions, to carry on with day-to-day stuff. Especially if you have a lot of things from the past, or if you have stuff that's happening now. But God always has a way to speak to you. He'll encourage you and carry you through.

I feel close to the Lord now. Like if I'm doing something around the house, the Holy Spirit is always whispering something. Or I just have, kind of like, "aha" moments, or moments when I feel this sort of tingly warmth and I get a sense of his peace.

What are your plans for the future?

Well, I believe I'm meant to be a teacher. I'm meant to be with kids. So I'm a preschool teacher now, and eventually I'd like to earn my bachelor's degree in early childhood education. It's going to take a while because I'm a Mom and I have a job, but that's where I'm headed.

Do you have any final thoughts?

If you look on the map, Russia is a really big country. And out of a small town, out of nowhere really, God plucked me out and brought me here. And I belong to this family. I know that now. They are going to love me and stand by me, no matter what.

I think God wants that for all of us. Wherever we are, he sees us. We can know that we belong to his family, that he loves us and he's going to stand by us, no matter what.

Vijay's Story

From the age of ten or eleven, I was addicted to porn. I was a Christian, right? But I couldn't wait to finish my prayer time to see that stuff. I'm so glad to be free! The guilt and shame, they really tear you apart.

I've heard people say addiction can be anything we do, so that we don't have to deal with the pain in our lives. Do you think that's true?

Absolutely! You know, we talk about addiction like it's only alcohol, drugs, porn. And those are terrible things. But I also know people who are addicted to gossip. To jealousy. To bickering. Those things also cause harm. If you think, I can't come to God until I break the addiction, it's stupid. Bring your addiction to God, just the way you are. He's going to accept you just the way you are. When you're honest, God will help you. We're just not transparent enough. Secondly, realize that you don't have the strength on your own. You need somebody here on earth, somebody with a healed heart, to talk to.

What was the pain you were avoiding?

Several things. My Dad was a good dad, but he was a workaholic and a churchaholic. If somebody in the church needed help, he had energy for them, but not for me. It felt like a very personal rejection. There were many other people I had trouble forgiving. There were a lot of people I hurt, as well. Then I was just squeezed by life. For example, I was suspended from the University for something I didn't do. I held grudges, and I kept asking God: "Why did you let me go through this?" Remember, not everyone has the same personality.

We can react differently to what is said, to what happens to us. With my personality, these things matter to me.

What did it feel like, living with all that, and what did it do to you?

It's like you've got a backpack full of concrete blocks, and you're carrying it all day long. It feels so heavy. You keep piling people in your bag and you never deal with it.

I was like a vacuum cleaner, sucking up all the love and attention from everybody around me. You expect love. You demand love. But it's like there's a hole inside of you, so you can't keep love. It always leaks out. I made myself such a stubborn, hard, knuckleheaded person, so full of pride, that I came across like I was the biggest kahuna on this earth.

When did things start to change?

About five or six years ago, I heard someone talk about forgiveness. He said, if you had problems with your biological dad, that hinders you from seeing what your father in heaven looks like. And I just cried my eyes out. It felt like that moment was just for me. I had told others many, many times that God is our "Abba" daddy, but that was the first time I experienced what it really felt like. That was really something else.

From there, a full inner healing process began. It was very intense. I worked with a counselor. At first I felt so angry. I punched a lot of pillows. I wrote a letter to my Dad—I wasn't supposed to mail it, just get it all out—and it was 25 pages long. I had to learn about forgiveness. You cancel people's debts, what they owe you. That's what forgiveness is about. You don't hold them accountable, you

271

release them. I forgave twenty or thirty people like that. And God helps you to forgive yourself. He forgives you in an instant, but we want to keep reminding ourselves of everything we did. I eventually realized that I had to forgive God, too. It's not that he did anything wrong. It's just that we hold him accountable for things that happened to us, whether he did them or not, and we have to let that go.

That's amazing! How has it impacted your life?

Before, it was terrible. Really, you're living your life in bondage. The day I finally felt forgiven, I didn't know I could live like that! I didn't know I could smile like that. I'm not even a sinner anymore, because all my sins have been forgiven. Now I can look at myself in the mirror and say, "I'm an awesome child of God."

It's like a cycle. You forgive God, and you receive his love, so you're able to forgive yourself. Then you can love him back, and in return, you feel even more loved. His love stops leaking out, so you can retain it. You get to the point that you don't have anything to hide anymore. You can just be yourself. You can love the Father, you can love yourself, and you can freely love other people. You learn how to take responsibility, you forgive, you ask for forgiveness. Now, my wife and I are teaching our kids how to live like this. Live your life happy, you know?

Has anything about this journey been disappointing for you?

In my case there were people I'd hurt. I could say I was sorry and treat them differently, and I did, but some of them didn't want to see how I'm not that way anymore. And I need to be able to forgive them for that. They can say whatever they want; it's my decision what I make out of those words. I tried and tried to work it out. Ultimately, though, we decided that I needed some new friends.

Do you see forgiveness as a big, one-time moment or as a lifestyle?

Forgiveness is a lifestyle. It's not, like, you do this once and you're done. There are times I still ask, God, you really love me, right? There are times I need to forgive myself again. And forgiving other people, it's a neverending story, and it's not always easy. But remember that forgiveness is a decision. It's by choice, not by feeling. I don't want to be in bondage anymore. It's not worth it. Once you know what it's like, having no blocks in your backpack, you don't want any more blocks. When a new one shows up, you want to deal with it. I don't want my freedom to be taken away again.

Just last week I was getting really mad, and God showed me a picture. He kind of zooms out and shows me that this big hurt is only a tiny dot in my whole life. Then he zooms back in, and I realize, I'm chewing on something I don't need to chew. It's only temporary, you know? I need to let it go. God has so much more for me, but you cannot embrace it unless you release the hurt. It's like a rubber band that keeps pulling you back. I want to have an unoffendable heart. That's where I'm headed.

What would you say to someone who is struggling?

First, you need to know who you are in Christ. You're a born-again creation. God showed me that if you don't forgive yourself, then you have denied his sacrifice on the cross. You're making yourself bigger than him. It's like you never experienced the cross at all, or only halfway. God loves you and he forgives you. You have to accept that.

If you're caught up in a big sin, you have to know that anything you do in darkness, you're never going to come out of it. So you always need at least one person to be there for you and hold you accountable. There's a secret to confession. I think you're saying to a friend, I want to confess that Jesus is going to be Lord in the area of my addiction. That's when you become free.

If you're tied up in guilt and shame, then your whole heart isn't available to love. Love doesn't hold anything back, it's wholehearted. I'd say we're [meant to be] like a piece of love. So do what it takes to get free.

The biggest lie of the devil is when he tells you that you can never be free. God really does set you free. When he does, it's just phenomenal!

"Tula's" Story*

The night of my high school graduation party, my boyfriend got into a fight. By dawn, he'd been charged with murder. It was like a living nightmare, and the shame was almost unbearable. One day I was drawing pictures of wedding dresses, and the next day I was thinking about ways I could kill myself. I'd worked so hard to have this perfect image— the perfect Christian, the straight A student— so nobody would look too closely and see how broken I actually was on the inside. Now it was like the covers had been pulled back, and everybody could see that it was all a lie.

I felt desperate. My future hardly seemed like it was worth living for, but it turns out that God had other plans.

Tell me how it all began.

Do you know about the movie *Cinderella*? I remember watching it for the first time as a little girl, and just being transfixed. I thought, "I want to be like her when I grow up." To feel beautiful, to be wanted and loved and pursued by someone because you mattered to them, that would have meant everything to me. But for a long time, my life wasn't like that. I was more like the girl who was living in the ashes.

Life at my house was chaotic and stressful. By the time I was born,

---

* Not her real name.

Mom had four kids under the age of five, and both of her parents had died not too long before. She'd had a hard life and she drank a lot to cope with her pain. I don't remember her ever hugging me or saying, "I love you." At that time, she was unpredictable, mean, and nasty, and you walked on eggshells around her.

So I stayed out of the house a lot. While I was playing at a local church, I met the janitor and he became my "friend." He started luring me further and further into the back rooms. After that, our relationship turned into something very different, and it made me into someone very different. When I was eight years old, my dream of becoming Cinderella died. I knew that nobody like me was ever going to be anyone's princess.

From that point on, I was sure about two things: I was a very, very bad little girl, and nobody could ever know about the things I had done. Nobody could ever know who I really was. Looking back, that was the point where I started living a lie.

What did that look like for you?

On the outside, it looked like perfection. I didn't think you would like me unless I was perfect, and I was so desperate to be loved. Desperate, really, to feel like I was enough. Performing and perfection were just the mechanisms I used, and if they gave out Academy Awards to kids, I would've been a contender. As a child, I became the best girl, the A+ student, the teacher's pet. Once I became a teenager, I looked and acted like I had it all together. I never left the house unless I was dressed just right, and my hair and makeup were always perfect.

By the time I graduated from college, I thought I had it all figured out. I was a CPA and I was ambitious. I was the first one to get to the office and the last one to leave. I was tall and thin, and as well put-together as I could manage to be. Then on the weekends I partied hard, doing everything I could to have a good time. I was a star performer. I knew how to look and act like a success.

Did you feel like a success?

No, not at all! I felt like a fake, and keeping my mask in place all the time was exhausting. It was like trying to put a Band-Aid on wet skin. It didn't stick, and it couldn't really fix the ways I was broken.

Beneath the surface, here's what was really happening: I laughed when other people laughed, and I cried when they cried, but I didn't actually feel what they felt. It's like I was a stranger, watching my own life from the outside. I imitated other people so I could fit in, but it wasn't real. I knew I couldn't let the mask slip, not even for a second. I couldn't let anyone get too close. I was terrified that they might find out that my perfect image was a lie.

When I was sixteen I became a Christian, but I didn't really understand what had just happened to me. I knew God had wiped my slate clean, but now I thought it was up to me to keep it clean. How on earth was I going to do that? In a way, it made life even harder. Before, I'd only had to perform for other people. Now I started performing for God, as well.

My senior year in high school, I fell for a guy and thought he was "the one." But he went to a party, got in trouble, and ended up going to prison for murder. I went to see him in prison every weekend for three years, until the day he told me that he didn't see me being a part of his future. Talk about the ultimate rejection! When I broke up with him, I was so hurt that I sort of broke up with God, too, and I ran the other way into a wild lifestyle. I bailed out on my next fiancé just ten days before our wedding.

It's like I was two different people, the high achiever I presented to the world, and the dirty, broken wreck that I was so afraid for anyone to see. When I looked in the mirror, I hated the person I saw. The fact is that I was exhausted, terrified, and lonely. I didn't have any real friends.

How did you keep going?

It takes a lot of work to live a double life like that. In my case, it also took a whole lot of alcohol. And I could only let people get just so close before I'd start to think: I'm in trouble. You're going to find out who I really am. So about every two years, I'd change everything. Change the relationship, change the friendships, change the job. When I eventually met Rick, he's the first one who saw enough of the real "me" to encourage me to go to counseling. I'm not sure I was sold on the process, but I went anyway. I just wanted to get well enough for somebody to finally marry me, because I was afraid of ending up alone.

Tell me about that.

When I met the counselor, it was the first time I'd tried taking my mask off long enough to be real with another person. As he learned more about my life and my problems, he told me that beneath my sense of unworthiness, promiscuity, and drinking, I was hiding a deep sense of shame. For the first time, I began to think: maybe I wasn't just a really bad girl. Maybe I was broken. That didn't fix me, but at least I understood myself better. I had some cubbyholes I could put things away in, and I could function. I got well enough to make it down the aisle with Rick, and we started going back to church. Then I put the good Christian girl mask back on, doing all the things I thought you were supposed to do.

When did that change for you?

Someone at church invited me to a women's retreat focusing on the Song of Solomon. That was weird! The night before, I had opened my Bible at random and stumbled across that book for the first time. Then I'd accidentally come across my old wedding dress in the back of the closet.

I couldn't figure out why church people would talk about the Song of Solomon, though. It seemed totally inappropriate for the Bible, to me. So she explained it. "It's a beautiful love story, but it's also an analogy. Each one of us is like the Shulamite woman. God doesn't care what your background is. He loves you. He makes you beautiful, and you become the perfect, spotless bride who is worthy of his Son."

That's when the room started to swim, and I got very dizzy. It was like an earthquake took place in my soul. I'd spent my whole life in hiding, but the God of the Universe had found the real me. He actually saw me, and he told me what I'd needed to hear my whole life! I had never believed I was beautiful, and I certainly knew that I wasn't spotless. Three times engaged, could barely make it to the altar, no right to wear a white dress, yet God was calling me a

279

beautiful, spotless bride. That was the first time I'd ever been aware that God was speaking to me. I didn't even know he still did that. I thought you just read your Bible, because it told you what you were supposed to do. I never imagined that it showed you who you were going to become.

But God's words are alive, and when he speaks them directly to us, they have power. In that moment it felt like God was pouring balm over the wounds in my soul, and I was undone. I finally understood. This life wasn't about my performing for God. He loved me, and he was pursuing me. He wanted to have a relationship with me.

Tell me more about God pursuing you.

A friend invited me to join her for an intensive two-week course on uncovering and healing inner pain. One day I volunteered to be the class guinea pig, and the leader told me to ask Jesus if there was a specific memory he wanted to talk to me about. Immediately a picture came into my mind, and I remember thinking, "No, not that one." I was mortified.

You see, God reminded me about a day when the janitor had locked me in a closet. The priest came in to get supplies, and I could hear him muttering to himself. He was confused because he couldn't open the door. He had no idea that I was cowering behind it, terrified of being found out. In that moment I had experienced an overwhelming sense of shame, absolute terror and vulnerability. Now, it felt like all the years had been taken away, and it was happening to me in real time. I was sitting there, totally hysterical, bawling my eyes out.

I could vaguely hear the voice of the lady who was running the session. She said that I needed to ask, "Where are you, Jesus?" So I did.

I flashed back, and I could still hear the priest on the other side of the door. I could hear the keys rattling, as the janitor pretended to try to find the right one. Then I heard Jesus walking towards the door. He came closer and closer, and I felt more and more afraid. When I was eight, the priest never could get the door to open. This time, though, I knew that I was going to be found out.

Then suddenly the door burst open, and Jesus was there. He didn't hesitate for a second. He just bent down, picked me up in his arms, and gently said, *Oh, little one.* Then he carried me away.

Jesus wasn't mad at all! He was just so sad that this had happened to me. All those years I'd been hiding my real self from God, when all he wanted to do was rescue me. The fear and shame were gone, because I'd been enfolded in the arms of Jesus. I was safe. I was protected. I was loved. There are no words to describe what that felt like! Utter relief. Complete peace. That's the closest I can come to it.

Then the lady who was running the session said, "The Lord is telling me to do something now." She knelt down and acted like she was tenderly, carefully putting shoes on my feet. And suddenly I knew exactly why. I remembered my long-lost dream of being Cinderella. My prince, Jesus, had taken me out of the ashes. His servant was fitting the perfect glass slippers onto my feet.

Living in the YES!

What did that do in your life?

The Lord broke the power of shame off of me. It's is an evil, evil device that the enemy uses to keep us in bondage, to keep us believing that we're ugly and useless and worthless. When we experience shame, we want to hide from God, when the thing we need most of all is the Father's embrace. Shame stands outside the door of the Father's house and blocks the way. It looks down on us and says, "You can't come in." I hate shame so much. God must hate it even more than I do.

Is there an opposite experience to shame?

Yes. Perfect love. Not that you're loving God perfectly, but that's the way he loves you.

My childhood view of God had been pretty messed up. Somehow I'd gotten the idea that God the Father was really angry. I'd thought Jesus was like the good older brother, and he was standing between me and the wrath of God. But that isn't true at all, and I was about to find it out in a very personal way.

One day, Rick and I had gone to our small group, and not many people were there. It came out that I hadn't ever felt the love of God the Father. They asked me to kneel on the floor, and they prayed for Father God to show me how he saw me. That's when another memory came to mind.

I was eight years old, and I was at church for my first communion. All the other girls were wearing pretty white dresses with gloves. Their hair was done up, and they were wearing tiaras, but not me. My dress was plain and my hair was short. I felt ugly on the outside, and even uglier on the inside. Then God the Father walked into my memory. He knelt down in front of me, and I couldn't see his face, but I could see his beard and the nubby white linen of his robe. I reached out towards him, but I couldn't feel anything. It was like I had been locked out of my own life. I wasn't describing any of that out loud. It's just what I saw in my mind's eye.

Then my husband's voice broke in. He said, "Tula, I can see you in my mind. You look like you're seven or eight years old and you're wearing a white dress. I see the Father, and he's kneeling down in front of you on one knee. He's touching your eyes, and he's saying, 'You're so beautiful. I'm giving you new eyes so you can see yourself the way I see you.'"

In that moment, this sort of knowing came to me in a flash, and my old, false image of God the Father was blown to smithereens. I suddenly understood what the Bible means when it says that Jesus is the perfect representation of the Father. Jesus is kind, because God the Father is kind. They're alike. They had worked together to save me, and now they were working together to set me free. And I looked beautiful to God!

That's what he did. He chose my darkest day. He came to the ugliest, most broken place in my life to tell me how much he loved me, even then. That's where I began to experience his love for the first time. God wasn't pretending that I was something I wasn't. He didn't have to look at me through the blood of Jesus, so that he could stand the sight of me. Instead, he saw ME, all of me, just as I was, and he truly loved me.

How has that affected you?

That experience changed my life. I'd lived all my life with so much pain. I knew how to look like a success. I could make people think I was smart and even special, but nothing I did changed the awful rejection and shame I felt inside. Now all of that is different.

I've stopped feeling like I'm two different people. I don't pretend that I'm perfect anymore, and I don't need to hide my flaws. Instead, I think I'm becoming the person God always intended for me to be. He truly accepts me right where I am, and because of that, I can accept myself. I don't have to sit across the table from somebody and wear a mask to hide my real self. I don't have to perform in order to win God's approval. My work doesn't define my value. From the moment when I finally saw the way God looked at me, I knew: I have value, because I am loved. And I'm more connected with other people. Even my Mom! She became a Christian, and now she's on her own journey with God.

Do you ever feel ashamed anymore?

Sometimes shame still tries to get a voice in the narrative in my head. It's an old voice, a very familiar voice, but it's one that's growing fainter. If I make a mistake, or it those old feelings get stirred up, now I handle that differently. I don't have to hide or run away. I call a friend, and I turn to the Lord. It's really just going to be another opportunity for me to come to God and say, "Help me understand what's going on." I don't have to be perfect for him to love me, and because he does love me, he'll walk with me through a situation and help me to grow. Then the whole process turns out to be constructive rather than destructive.

What would you say to someone who's living like you were?

Find a place where you can take the mask off and stop pretending, because God loves you right where you are. You are loved, and it's safe to be seen. Seek out good counseling, one hundred percent. Inner healing, one thousand percent. Figure out which people are safe in your life. They're the ones who won't blow you off, but they won't coddle you, either. You can't do it alone. At the end of the day, we need each other. And remember that your wounds can't define you. Yes, they're part of your story, but they're not your whole story. God thinks you're beautiful! You're loved with an everlasting love, and nothing you do can change that. So let God in, and let him start healing you.

What does life look like for you now?

To me, Romans 8:15 in The Message gives us the perfect description of life with God. It says, "This resurrection life you received from God is not a timid, grave-tending life. It's adventurously expectant, greeting God with a childlike 'What's next, Papa?'" That's how we get to live. Adventurous, trusting, expectant. Some things will be hard, but he'll be there by our side, through them and in the midst of them.

Would you pray for someone who's reading the book?

Father God, whoever is reading this book right now, in the name of Jesus, would you just come and kneel down in front of them the way you knelt in front of me? Give them what they need at this moment in time. Whether it's safety, or comfort, or love, or acceptance, just let them see themselves being gathered up into your big, huge, mighty, powerful arms, so that they feel a Father's embrace. Let them feel the warmth of your hug and feel your breath on their cheek as you whisper, "I love you, precious one. I will never leave you. I'm so sorry for what you've been through. I will always be with you as you go through this journey." Lord, destroy the lies that have kept them in bondage. Destroy the bars of shame, of pain. Bring healing and freedom into their lives. I bless them as your very own beloved sons and daughters, in Jesus' name, Amen.

Melissa's Story

Life changed for me one night when my daughter Bella was very sick. She had severe food allergies. Vomiting, seizures, trips to the hospital. This time she was curled up on the bathroom floor in a fetal position screaming, 'Help me, Mommy! Please help me!' It was absolutely horrific. I felt like I was going to die because I couldn't help my child, and I was desperate. I'd been asking, 'Where are you, God? Your Word says there's no sickness in heaven. You healed everybody in the Bible. Why is my child sick?'

That night, the Lord told me exactly how to pray for her. He told me to put my hands on her stomach, command it to stop, and clap. That felt odd, but it was like a parent saying, 'I need you to do this NOW.' When I did what he said, she stood up immediately and said, 'It's gone!' And it was. We went downstairs, got pots and pans and started banging them while we danced around, just praising Jesus. Since then she has been extremely healthy, no more problems. And over the next eighteen months, my other kids were healed as well.

What did healing look like for them?

My two older kids also had severe food allergies, and they were healed over time. Then there's my youngest, Christiano. When he was about a year old, he stopped standing up and started crawling again. We had extensive tests done. Eventually one of the top specialists in the United States told us, "Your son has the worst case of juvenile rheumatoid arthritis that I have ever seen. He will never have a normal life."

We went home, gave him his medicine, and prayed. I spoke Scripture over him and told his legs what they were going to do. "Your legs have the strength of an ox. You're going to run with perseverance." We prayed and kept praying. Our friends prayed, and our pastor anointed him with oil. And he was healed! I can't point to a specific moment when we saw it happen, like we did with Bella. He just got better.

Now he's completely well. No more symptoms, no more medicine. And he runs! He actually just got scouted by a professional soccer team because he's one of the fastest kids, and it's just amazing.

What is life like now for all of you now?

Oh, John 10:10, abundant living. My kids can go to parties and eat normal foods. They play sports, they're not on any medication, they only take vitamins, and they are rarely ever sick. There's nothing wrong with their stomachs, there's nothing wrong with their vision, they are perfectly healthy. We have freedom. Praise God! I don't have to worry. I don't even think about it anymore. But I do have compassion for other people who do, and I have a heart to pray for others.

Tell me more about your experience with prayer and healing.

I developed a huge passion to see God heal. I started reading a lot of materials on healing, and everything in my spirit just welled up. What did they do in the Bible? How did they pray? I just literally ate and slept and thought, *healing*. I would meet somebody, and their kids would be gluten-free, dairy free, wheat free, and I would say, "Let me tell you what God did for me." He set me free, he set my children free, and he will do the same for them. God is no respecter of persons, seriously.

Now a righteous anger rises up in me when I see that the Liar has done that to somebody else, and I'm constantly asking people, 'Can I pray for you?' Sometimes it will be just a headache. I have also seen God heal deaf ears, I've seen him heal broken bones. An older man from church had been deaf in his left ear, I think it was for about half his life, and God healed him about four weeks after we prayed together.

Another time, my son Anthony got carried off the soccer field and it looked like his leg was broken. His knee was swollen to twice its normal size and contorted. He couldn't even hobble, and he was in so much pain. But we were praying all the way to the hospital. I told the bones to do whatever a doctor would do. *"Bones, align. Flesh, align. Kneecap, go back in place."*

When we got to the hospital, I saw my husband Ken put Anthony in the wheelchair. Then Anthony looks up at his father and down at his knee. He stands up and starts jumping up and down, up and down, and he says, "It's gone!" Both his knees were completely normal. So I crossed his name off the waiting list and we went home to have a party with our family. It was an absolute miracle. Complete healing!

At this point, I have prayed for so many kids on the soccer field. It can look like they are on the way to the hospital, and God heals them right then and there. It just fills me with joy every time I see God do that. It's such a beautiful demonstration of who he is.

Does everyone you pray for get healed?

No. I wish they did! But they can always experience the love of the Father, and that's so important. There was this one instance where I prayed for a young man and his arm was healed. The next week something else happened. He was not healed, and I was upset.

I asked the Lord, "What are you doing?" and he told me, "I want you to love them. Bring them dinner." As it turns out, it was a different kind of healing. Nobody had ever done anything like that for them.

You have a strong faith. Did you grow up in a Christian home?

No. I didn't grow up going to church. Before the age of nineteen, I was a party girl. I liked to do fun things, and everything was about me. It was like being on a gerbil wheel, racing constantly. 'What do they think of me? Did I say this right? Did I do this right?' But then my best friend got saved and I watched her life change. The Holy Spirit just drew me in. One night at one o'clock in the morning, I walked down to her house and knocked on her door and said, "I want what you have."

I was instantly changed, the very next day. I felt light, I felt clean, I felt vibrant. I wanted to wake up every morning. I felt that I had purpose and meaning. The way I dressed, the things I said, the things I listened to, my desires completely changed. I didn't want the things that I had wanted just the week before. I no longer had things in common with my party friends. I just wanted more of Jesus.

Wanting more of Jesus. What does that look like for you?

I love being connected to God. I'm living nonstop in a relationship with him, continually. I'm talking to him. He's talking to me. I'm asking him, 'Lord, what do you want to say to me?' and I'm listening. I'm asking, 'What are you doing? How can I cooperate with that? Is there somebody you want me to love on?" He whispers, "I want you to love on this person by making them a meal. I want you to love on that one by encouraging them." And I do the things he asks me to do.

Over time, I've learned that 'being spiritual' is not a feeling. It isn't based on what I do; it's who I am. Whether I'm driving my kids someplace, or spending time with a friend, or digging in my garden, it's all for God's glory. The Holy Spirit lives in my body. He's with me, and he goes with me wherever I am. I can literally walk into the midst of chaos and still feel his peace. My life can be busy and complicated. Sometimes it feels like my family of six is going in a hundred different directions. But I've discovered that I carry the Lord's presence with me wherever I go. That's what I want to be—a carrier. I carry his glory! Whether I'm at church, or the grocery store, or the soccer field, the Lord is there with me. That's his promise to every believer. He wants to do life with us.

Do you actually feel his presence all the time?

No. But I know he's with me all the time, because that's what he promised. Sometimes I feel his presence and I hear his still, small voice deep in my heart, leading me. Sometimes in a situation I just know what he thinks, because I've spent so much time with him. Sometimes I have to pray and wait. Whatever happens, I know I don't have to do things in my own strength anymore. I turn to him. I get to be connected to him.

What would you say to someone who wants to be closer to God?

Find a friend and pray together. Read the Word. Find a good church home. Find people you can connect with. Put on a worship song and just lay back and receive. There are so many different ways to connect with God. It's not that you have to do all these things at once. But which one do you think you could do now? Just try it.

Do you have any other thoughts you like to share?

The verse that comes to mind is, "I can do all things through Christ who strengthens me." No matter where anyone is in their walk with God, Christ is the one who gives them strength. He gives them strength in their marriage. Is it strength in parenting? Is it strength to find their faith again? Is it the strength to keep going? Just keep turning to him.

And be encouraged! The kind of life I live is available to every believer. What God has done for me, he'll do for all of us.

Mario, Marlene, & Eder's Story

Tell me more about how you started praying for food.

Marlene: There were so many times when we had nothing to eat. That was when God started working with my faith and making it stronger. The first time that happened, I stayed up and prayed all night. In the morning, I woke my kids and told them to start praying, too. We really had nothing, you know? And somebody came and brought us groceries. That happened so many times, I can't tell you.

Eder: (laughs) So many times! One time, it was really funny. Mom went to her room to pray for food, and she was praying for a long time. While she was there, one of her friends came to our house and opened the fridge, and she saw it was empty. So she went to the store and bought food for us. Then she came back and put it all in the fridge, and she left. When Mom came out, she didn't know what to do. It looked like shrimp and fruit and all sorts of really nice stuff had just appeared while she was praying! That's just one example of how we've always seen what God can do. We've seen him do so many miracles, physical healing, emotional healing, provision.

You both had such challenges in your early lives. Tell me more.

Mario: Before I was born, my Mom tried to abort me three times, but the Lord saved me. They were so poor, and she thought she already had too many kids. She didn't know what to do with one more. Then one time in church, the Pastor said, "God wants to heal someone who was rejected by their Mom before they were born," and God healed my heart. My Mom confessed everything when she was dying, and I forgave her. We made peace. And I lived a bad life before I was a

293

Christian. I was in a lot of accidents, in cars and on the job. God protected me again and again.

Marlene: I was raised by my aunt, and I can't tell you how poor we were. We had nothing. In our country, high school isn't free, and nobody would pay for me to study, but I got a scholarship. That's how I got an education. That was the first miracle I had seen. As a girl, I felt a lot of emptiness because I had been raised by an aunt, and I never had the love of a mom or a dad. When I became a Christian, something amazing happened. I felt God's presence, and I cried and cried. It was the first time I had felt the love of a Father. And before my Mom died, God reconciled my family.

Mario, some amazing things happened while you were on the ships?

Mario: First of all, my going at all was a miracle. In that moment when I had no work and no money, the Lord gave me two visas from the US Embassy. That just never happens! If one visa is hard to get, the second is even harder. They gave me a tourist/work visa, and also a transit visa. That's how I was able to fly to the ship in Europe, and then later I worked for the US Navy.

God saved me so many times. Three times, I was on a ship in the worst kind of storms, with waves that were up to fifteen meters high, and we didn't sink. One time I was on a platform in the Gulf of Mexico, and I happened to look up just as a huge, twenty-four-inch diameter pipe came crashing down. I jumped to the side and wasn't hurt, but I was so scared to think that my life depended on only three seconds. There were so many situations like that. Another time, my back was injured. I was in so much pain that I could hardly move. But I prayed, and God healed me.

294

You had a family member who was healed, right?

Eder: Mom's younger sister got very sick, and we took her in. We had to do everything for her, like she was a baby. Mom was like, "What have I done? How can I feed her, when I can hardly feed my own children?" But Mom knew only one thing: that the core of everything is Jesus.

Mom was praying, asking God to help her sister. The Lord told her to write down questions and show them to my aunt. And my aunt would answer, "uhhh," or "uhhh uhhh." When she felt like the question was too much, she would start screaming, "Noooooooo!" But over time, her story came out. God started healing her and making her feel loved. You can hardly imagine it. She had been like a zombie. But in thirty days, she became a normal person again! It was a huge testimony, because all of us kids were involved. It was completely a mess, but God exchanged our messiness for his glory.

Marlene: God restored so much from that point. Nobody in my family had ever been a Christian, except for one cousin. But after this, they all started becoming Christians. Now my sisters are pillars of the church. And God gave me the money, and I was able to build new houses for all my sisters, and make sure all their kids went to the University. The blessings that fell onto us, fell onto all of our family as well.

It sounds like there are so many ways you've seen God's kindness.

Marlene: Yes! Here's another example. I used to only have two dresses [*one to wash and one to wear*]. One time I was at church praising the Lord, and I saw a woman wearing a beautiful dress. I

295

thought, *Oh, I wish I could be dressed like that.* But I stopped right away and thought, *My Lord, I'm so sorry.* And I kept praising the Lord. I forgot about it. Then, a few days later, someone brought me a dress! It meant so much to me, right in that moment. It really built my faith.

Now people send us big boxes of clothes, shoes, everything. We give them away to everybody, even the people who are off in the mountains.

Sometimes in a church service, we see people who have been starving for days, and we share food with them. A lot of churches only ask for money, but God has blessed us, and we give to people. Now they are learning how to give to God.

We teach people how to be generous in other ways, too. Jesus loves all of us. When two people don't like each other, we help them to understand that their problems are nothing, and that we have to be very loving to each other. So now, there are a lot of testimonies among the brothers. They'll say, "I didn't used to like that man, but now, I like him."

Oh, and I have to tell you this! Back when we had nothing, when I was walking and praying in my room, I would start feeling the glory of God descending. I wanted to show God how much I loved him. So I used to play "air guitar," and I would sing to the Lord. I told him that I wished I knew how to play an instrument, but I couldn't. And do you know what's the most beautiful thing? He gave me two musicians! Marito plays viola, and Eder plays oboe. They've both studied at famous conservatories. Now, when they're at home, they play and I sing with them. I praise the Lord, because they are such a gift in my life.

Eder, what is happening in your life?

Eder: At this point, I'm at a place in my life where a lot of changes are happening. I have a graduate fellowship to study oboe in the US, and I'm in national music competitions. I get invited all over the place with all my expenses paid. What God is doing, it's just amazing. I grew up in a house made of dirt, and the floor was sand, you know? But what isn't changing is my faith in God. I still believe, just like a little kid. I'm very naïve with him. He tells me something, and I'm like, "Really? Wow!" And I believe it. And then I just take a moment, and he fills me with his presence. He does things. I'm literally doing everything by his grace.

After all the years we've seen the glory of God just working like *this (snaps his fingers)* ... I think everyone in my family understands one thing. If we only believe in him and obey him, we're going to have everything. Not because we want it, but because we're looking for him first.

Sometimes people can say bad things over all of us, but it's okay. God loves to prove them wrong. When that happens, I just go to my room and pray, and I put everything in his hands.

I can be so far out of my comfort zone, but it's okay. I don't feel fear, because God is everywhere, so I'm still with God. I just feel peaceful and excited to see what he has next. I feel like that's what it's like to be a son of God. In the end, that's what life is about: enjoying God, so that we can enjoy everything else. It's God, it's God, and it will always be the Lord. I think those are the basics that keep me up straight, that keep me secure.

Living in the YES!

What would you say to someone who feels discouraged?

Marlene: I understand that. I was rejected. I was abandoned. I was criticized. I was told so many bad things. But now the word of Isaiah 61 has been accomplished, and God has exchanged all of that for such good things. Now I only have to give the glory to God, and serve him. I tell about all my miseries so that others can have hope, that God is going to restore, that God is going to do things that are beyond your comprehension. God is going to accomplish his purpose.

Now I don't worry about anything. If it's raining in the morning, well, let it rain! If there's a very hot day, well, just put on some sunscreen. There is nothing man can do to avoid whatever God wants to do. The more we trust him, the less we suffer.

What do you say to someone who is in a very difficult situation?

Marlene: That they should not lose hope in God. What he promises is going to come. We try to build that into their hearts, into their souls, into their spirits. We teach them how to live, so that they try to live in integrity, that they are honest with themselves and with God. Then you pray! And you keep praying until God answers you. You don't give up. God wants us to have conviction that he is the Lord, even if we don't see him. If you're facing a struggle, he doesn't want you to suffer. He wants you to pass the test. He wants to give you that "100!" As you wait for the answer, read the Bible—the Word of God is alive—pray to the Lord, and spend time with your brothers and sisters.

Mario: Then we try to help them with something material as they wait for the answer to come.

Eder: It's like when the soil is very dry and cracked. Then God comes and he waters, and you see how things start having more life. We have seen God do that, exactly like that, in the lives of so many people.

Your life can look like a puzzle that has been all destroyed. God is the one who starts picking up the pieces and putting them together. My advice is to be naïve towards God. Trust him. He can pick up every single piece. In the end, when the pieces are all put together, what you're going to see will be his glory.

Would you pray for someone who's in a desperate situation?

Eder: Father, I believe that your purpose is to restore and to bring back to life. For those who feel like they are at the bottom of the heap, where all they see is loneliness, darkness, suffocation, help them to look up and see you. You are their rescuer. Thank you very much for all you have done, and for all you're planning to do. Come into their lives. Only you have all the tools to pick them up and bring them back to life. Restore everything they have lost and put them in places of high honor, so they can speak your truth. Then they, too, can bring hope to those who once lost it. In the Name of Jesus, Amen.

"Peter & Anne's" Story*

How did your life change after that first conference experience?

Anne: I realized that Jesus died for a lot more than I was taking advantage of. I was only partaking in forgiveness and a little bit of grace, when he died for my healing! For my abundance! For complete joy and peace and power in all circumstances, for his presence in our lives. I'd been leaving so much on the table. What a waste! I don't want to waste anything like that anymore.

We started having all kinds of adventures with God. For example, Peter's Dad had a stroke. While we were visiting with him, his roommate started moaning in agonizing pain. The next thing I know, I'm crossing the room, and I'm praying a simple, childlike prayer: 'In Jesus' name, I command this pain to go.' Ten minutes later he sat up in bed. He told me that he'd had a very painful COPD lesion on his lung, and all the pain had vanished the minute I prayed for him. Months later, he told me the pain had never returned.

And my neighbor Natalie was a tough older woman who'd moved here from New York City. One day we were sitting by her pool, and she asked if I believed in reincarnation. The Holy Spirit whispered: *Tell her that you don't believe in reincarnation, but you do believe in resurrection. Then shut up.* He kept telling me exactly what to say, in

---

* Not their real names.

300

little short snippets like that. After thirty minutes she said, 'I want to hear everything you know. Will you come back and tell me?'

Another time, this same neighbor had been in the hospital with a panic attack, and I called to pray with her over the phone. She started moaning: 'Ohhh! Ohhh! Ohhh!' Then she said, 'It's like somebody's pouring oil over my head, and the more you pray, it's getting hotter and hotter, and I feel such peace.' You can't imagine how strange that was. She'd never been around church or church people, and her personality was so hard. But she started changing. Four months later she accepted Christ. Two months after that, she fell and hit her head and died, but she died as a different person than the person she had been for most of her life.

Peter: Not every prayer we've prayed has been answered, or answered fully in the ways that we'd hoped for, but we have seen God do so many amazing things. We love praying for people.

Did this new kind of life touch you personally, as well?

Peter: Yes! Let me tell you about one of our experiences, hearing from God. We'd started going to a new church. One day the pastor told us to lean back, close our eyes, and think about whatever kept us awake at night. I thought about three things. We needed some cash flow, we had a family member who was struggling with addiction, and I felt depressed.

Then he said to ask God what he thinks about those things. Right away, this crawler or banner started scrolling across my mind's eye, like you might see for a TV news flash, and it read, 'Everything is going to be okay.' I was so startled! I asked God, 'Is that you?' I thought it was the sort of thing I would tell myself, just to feel better. Then the banner changed. Now it said, 'Keep listening to the pastor, because he's about to say the word, uttermost.' And he did say it! I couldn't wait to tell Anne.

Anne: God's first answer came right away. By the time we got to the car, Peter's depression was gone. As for the other things, we prayed about them every morning. For the next four months, it felt very dark. None of our circumstances changed. But when one of us got overwhelmed, the other would say: 'No, no, no. What did God say? He said everything is going to be okay, and he confirmed it with uttermost. We can stand on that, we can believe it, and we're going to declare it.' Then we'd start thanking God as if it was already done. We practiced standing on that, and it built our faith up.

Peter: Here's what God did next. Anne had been praying that we could purchase another business like mine so we could improve our cash flow. On January first, out of the blue a guy calls me. He says that he lives nearby, he has a business like mine, and he's just gotten out of the hospital. He'd been so sick that his family was planning his funeral. Now he's made a miraculous recovery, but he wants to retire. Long story short, I go to see him the next day. While I'm there, he gives me his business, gives me his customer list, gives me all his tools and supplies, and promises to write a letter of recommendation to all his customers.

Before I left, I prayed for them, and they both started weeping because they were being affected by the Holy Spirit. They kept telling me how they thought I was a blessing to them. I'm like, "Are you kidding me? You just gave me your business, and you think I'm a blessing to you?"

And finally, this was the third thing we had asked God about. We kept praying for our family member. It was a tough time, and we almost lost them, but we kept standing on God's promise and uttermost. On January second, the same day the business was given to us, they started a new job. Now they're making such great progress, and doing really well.

How do you see life differently now?

Anne: I'm not going to say that I don't ever think that old way. 'Arrrgh! Can you believe we're going through this again?' And exasperation comes, and fear and all of that. But I spend less time in that frame of mind, and pretty quickly we both say, 'Let's pray about it. What is the lie that we're tempted to believe, either about ourselves, or the situation, or God, and what is the truth?' We declare what we believe to be true in this situation. Then we come together and pray over it frequently. We've learned how to stand in faith on the promises of God.

We don't feel as powerless as we did before, and there's an authority in our prayers. It's not that we're spared from pain and suffering, but when we walk through trials and difficulties, we've learned how to experience joy and peace in the middle of that. We've seen God redeem completely dark situations. Sometimes we still have to push back against unbelief, but we have so much more confidence and boldness about what God wants to do. Our expectations have changed and that fuels our faith.

What would you say to someone who's in the place where you were?

Peter: This is for you! We love getting unbelieving believers into a small group and sharing biblical proof as to why these things are true. We love sharing testimonies about what God has done, and we love being there when the Holy Spirit shows up for them. We've never looked back. I tell people: you can forget your house, your 401k, your IRA, your job. Nothing matters like this does. Whenever that liquid love is flowing through you, that's all you need. You can live on it. You can run on it.

Anne: Whatever you're facing, ask yourself: What has God already said in his Word, and how does it apply to where you are right now? Believe it. Stand on it. Call on him to fulfill his Word. Stop being paralyzed by anxiety and fear. You don't need to limit God based on your experience. Tell your experience to line up with God's Word, instead.

It's just hard to take it in, how generous God is. Be hungry for him, because there's so much more to this life than you know. That's what we started calling this experience: 'the more.' It's here for you, too. Ask him for more.

Would you pray for someone who's in that place right now?

Anne: Lord, I pray that we would all experience a hunger that cannot be satisfied with intellectual knowledge but can only be satisfied by you. Where cynicism has caused someone to smirk, cause it to be completely consumed by hope and faith. Where there has been distance from you, replace that with true connection to your Holy Spirit. Bring them intimacy and power, so that they're filled to overflowing. Let peace, joy, and righteousness be the fruit of their life.

Peter: Lord, we just pray that everyone who lays their hands on this book would be touched. That your Holy Spirit would well up within them, Lord. That they would sense a closer relationship to you. That they would be lifted, truth would be revealed, and they would begin to walk in the fullness of your Spirit that they never knew was available to them. We pray for supernatural healing, supernatural awareness of all your gifts. Lord, there is always more of you. Bring them to the more!

Living in the YES!

About The Author

Laura and her husband live in Atlanta, where they are active in their local church. When she's not writing or listening to other people's stories, she works part-time for a small software company. She enjoys traveling and spending time with her friends, kids, and grandkids.

Laura is no stranger to difficulty. The mother of a formerly "autistic" son and a formerly "emotionally-disabled" daughter, she herself is the survivor of a debilitating traumatic brain injury. Her family has seen God perform one astounding miracle after another. Yet she says that the greatest miracle was learning how to be connected to him, even in the middle of life's troubles. She passionately believes that this sort of life is available to everyone.

Their family includes both biological and adopted children, plus six honorary kids: former exchange students from across the globe who lived with them for a year each.

Laura holds degrees from Oral Roberts University (Communication) and Georgia State (MBA). Her varied career has included time as an accountant, information manager, stay-at-home Mom, and mural

307

artist. Her deepest passion is for encouraging others and seeing them become more connected to their destiny.

For more information please visit:

LauraBoal.com

LivingInTheYes.com

End Notes

[1] Romans 3:20-24

[2] Mark 9:23, Luke 18:27, Romans 8:31-39, 12:2

[3] This beautiful woman is not named in Scripture. I made up the name "Amara" for the sake of the story.

[4] God's majesty: Exodus 3:5-6; Isaiah 6:1-5; Daniel 8:15-17

[5] His love: 1 John 4:16

[6] You can find Joseph's story in Genesis, chapters 37-50

[7] Genesis 50:20

[8] John 10:10, MSG

[9] God's goodness: James 1:13, 17; Hebrews 13:5, TPT

[10] God is: faithful - Deuteronomy 7:9; loving - 1 John 4:8-10; good - Exodus 33:19; trustworthy - Psalm 33:4; unchanging - Numbers 23:19, Hebrews 13:8; powerful - Psalm 97:1-6; gentle - Isaiah 42:3; compassionate - Isaiah 53:4-5; joyful - Psalm 16:11; transcendent - Isaiah 40:25-26; he knows us - Jeremiah 1:5, Luke 12:7; respectful - Deuteronomy 30:19; fair - Psalm 89:14; unafraid of evil - Psalm 2:1-6, Revelation 20:7-10; effective - Isaiah 55:8-11; his invitation to us - Revelation 22:17

[11] The one thing: Haggai 2:7

[12] We will address the Old Testament Law in the next chapter. For a richer understanding of the Prophets, consider reading *The Message of the Prophets* by J. Daniel Hays.

[13] Hebrews 1:3

[14] Romans 8: 15, 38-39, 2 Corinthians 1:3-4, Philippians 1.6

[15] John 1:18, Hebrews 1:3

[16] Matthew 7:7; NLT particularly expresses the Greek verb form, "keep on asking"

[17] Matthew 6:10, paraphrased

[18] Ephesians 3:20

[19] 1 Peter 5:6-7

[20] Matthew 9:36

[21] Romans 8:28-39

[22] Jeremiah 29:11

[23] 1 Peter 2:2

[24] Philippians 2:13

[25] James 1:2-4, Romans 5:1-5

[26] John 14:18, Matthew 28:20

[27] Philippians 4:19, Ephesians 3:20

[28] Mark 10:18

[29] Genesis 3

[30] "Pharisees" were Jewish religious leaders who were experts at interpreting and keeping the law of Moses.

[31] Matthew 23

[32] Matthew 8:16, Mark 6:56, Luke 4:40, Matthew 11:2-5

[33] John 11:42, 17:11

[34] John 19:30

[35] Luke 22:20

[36] Romans 3:20

[37] Romans 3:21-23, Philippians 3:8-9

[38] Also see 1 Corinthians 2:7-8

[39] Luke 15:3-6, Jeremiah 31:3, 1 John 4:19

[40] Ephesians 2:4-5, Jeremiah 1:5a

[41] 1 John 4:9-10

[42] John 3:16-17, 17:23b

[43] Romans 5:8

[44] Ephesians 1:4-5

[45] John 15:15, Ephesians 2:19, 1 John 3:1

[46] Luke 24:13-32

[47] Hebrews 4:16, 10:22

[48] John 14:2-3, Luke 13:29, Revelation 19:9

[49] Swag bags: If you were an honoree at the Academy Awards or the Super Bowl, you would leave with a gift bag containing hundreds or thousands of dollars' worth of really nice stuff. What would be in the Holy Spirit's swag bag for you? Peace? Healing? Joy?

[50] Romans 3:23

[51] 2 Corinthians 5:17

[52] Jeremiah 31:33-34, Hebrews 10:16

[53] Ephesians 2:4, Colossians 2:13

[54] Hebrews 10:11-14, 19-22
[55] Ephesians 5:3, 25-27; Colossians 1:21-22, 3:12
[56] Romans 6:11, Colossians 2:11-14
[57] Romans 8:1-2
[58] John 15:5
[59] The Greek word which is often translated as "pruning" is actually *kathairō*, which means "to clean." A variation of the same word appears in the next sentence, when Jesus says, "The words I have spoken over you have already cleansed you." See the book *Secrets of the Vine* by Bruce Wilkinson for more
[60] John 17:3
[61] Hebrews 10:10
[62] 2 Corinthians 5:17-21
[63] 2 Corinthians 7:10
[64] Genesis 1:27, 2:7
[65] Genesis 3
[66] Ephesians 2:1
[67] John 3:16-18
[68] Philippans 2:5-11
[69] Isaiah 53:4-5, Matthew 8:16-17, 1 Peter 2:24
[70] Colossians 2:15
[71] John 20:1-17
[72] Hebrews 8:3-5, 9:11-14, 10:11-13
[73] "Put you to rights" is a Southern idiom. Imagine a child coming to his mother with a skinned knee. She hugs and comforts him, cleans the wound and bandages it, gives him a cookie, and sends him off with a smile as he runs back outside to play.
[74] Romans 3:21-24
[75] John 7:38
[76] Romans 5:15-21
[77] Colossians 2:9-10
[78] Philippians 3:4-9
[79] 1 John 5:12
[80] See footnote 75
[81] Hebrews 10:10-14, 19-23

[82] Ephesians 3:16-19

[83] John 10:4

[84] "El Shaddai" (Genesis 17:1) is generally translated as "[I AM] God Who Is More Than Enough"

[85] Hebrews 12:1-12

[86] John 17:3

[87] *The David* is a statue carved by Michelangelo in the sixteenth century. He stands seventeen feet (five meters) tall and is widely believed to be one of the greatest sculptures of all times.

[88] We talk about "love, peace and joy" as human attributes, and they are. Yet when those things come from God, they're so much more powerful that it almost seems foolish to use the same words. It would be like comparing a hand drill with power tools.

[89] 1 Corinthians 12:12-14

[90] Isaiah 6:3, 2 Corinthians 3:18

[91] Acts 17:6, 4:29-31

[92] Acts 1:8

[93] See John 16:13-14, 14:16-17, Acts 1:8, Luke 24:49

[94] Isaiah 59:20

[95] Isaiah 59:21

[96] Joel 2:28

[97] Matthew 4:1

[98] Luke 4:1

[99] Luke 4:14

[100] John 16:7, paraphrased

[101] John 3:8

[102] Romans 8:11

[103] John 14:16-17, 14:26-27; 15:26, 16:7-11. 16:13-14, Acts 1:8, 2:17, 2:38, 6:10, Romans 8:6-11,8:26-27, 1 Corinthians 2:9-13, 12:4,7, 2 Corinthians 1:21-22, 3:17-18, Galatians 5:22-23, Ephesians 1:17, Ephesians 3:20-21

[104] To learn more about the many different ways the Holy Spirit comes, read through the book of Acts.

[105] Randy Clark, *Baptized in the Spirit*, pp. 99-100

[106] 1 Kings 19:12

[107] Acts 2:2

[108] Matthew 5:14-16

[109] 1 Corinthians 12:4

[110] Matthew 3:16

[111] 1 Thessalonians 5:19; 2 Corinthians 7:10

[112] 2 Chronicles 6:12–7:3

[113] Hebrews 8:6

[114] 1 Peter 2:5

[115] Genesis 1:26; Genesis 2-3

[116] Revelation 4:1-2

[117] Philippians 2:5-11

[118] 2 Corinthians 3:2-3

[119] Galatians 4:4-7, Romans 8:14-17, 29

[120] Ephesians 6:10-17

[121] 1 Corinthians 2:6-7, Ephesians 4:11-15, James 1:2-4; Psalm 91:1

[122] "Put you to rights": See footnote 75.

[123] Jeremiah 2:13

[124] Layperson: a church leader who is not ordained clergy.

[125] 1 Peter 5:6-7; Isaiah 40:27-31

[126] Romans 8:34, 8:26-27, Hebrews 12:1-3

[127] Philippians 1:6

[128] Acts 10:34-43, John 17:3, 1 John 5:11-13